PRAISE FOR THE TAO OF ROWING WHITEWATER

"John French's brilliant writing has a beautiful, relatable clarity and a poetry that explains his growth-filled journey and puts you right in the boat with oars in hand, in the zone, in the flow, running the rapids. *The Tao of Rowing Whitewater* is a must read for all river guides – and also a perfect way for armchair adventurers to deeply imbibe the profound thrill, magic and soul-expanding adventure of rowing whitewater."

— WILLIAM MCGINNIS, AUTHOR OF
WHITEWATER RAFTING, THE GUIDE'S
GUIDE AUGMENTED: REFLECTIONS ON
PROFESSIONAL RIVER GUIDING, AND
THRILLER NOVELS INCLUDING
WHITEWATER: A THRILLER.

"To those willing to find parts of themselves they didn't know existed, take risks, embrace adventure, and discover new ways to navigate downstream, and new paths to being fully human, they will find John French a thoughtful, eager, deeply-spirited guide. *The Tao of Rowing Whitewater* delivers a soulful meditation on the nature of wild rivers and those who ride them, a kind of 21st century *Zen and the Art of Motorcycle Maintenance* exploring enlightenment while piloting a cataract-ready conveyance. ... John's lessons and musing are the next best thing to getting wet."

— RICHARD BANGS, AUTHOR AND CO-FOUNDER OF SOBEK EXPEDITIONS

"*The Tao of Whitewater* is a sublime mashup of river stories, instructional advice, and spiritual memoir. John French captures highs and lows of learning to run rivers and the exultation of feeling at home on whitewater and in sync with the flow. For the aspiring river guide, this slim volume is essential reading. And it will remind veteran boaters why they picked up a paddle or got behind the oars in the first place."

— MICHAEL SHAPIRO, AUTHOR, *A SENSE OF PLACE*

"This slim volume is a gem. There are clear instructions on how to read, run, and think about rivers. The prose, which flows fast and clear, is both amusing and illuminating."

— TIM CAHILL, AUTHOR OF JAGUARS RIPPED MY FLESH AND HOLD THE ENLIGHTENMENT

THE TAO OF ROWING WHITEWATER

LESSONS FROM RAFTING THE WORLD'S WILDEST RIVERS

JOHN FRENCH

COPYRIGHT

Paperback ISBN: 979-8-9923618-3-4

Ebook: ISBN: 979-8-9923618-2-7

The following chapters were previously published on Medium: *Whitewater Smackdown, Listen.*

The publisher and the author strongly recommend that you be in good physical condition to participate in rowing rivers. You should understand that when rowing whitewater, there is the possibility of physical injury. If you engage in running a river, you agree that you do so at your own risk, are voluntarily participating in these activities, assume all risk of injury to yourself, and agree to release and discharge the publisher and the author from any and all claims or causes of action, known or unknown, arising out of the contents of this book. The publisher and the author advise you to take full responsibility for your safety and know your limits. Make sure to maintain your equipment properly and do not exceed your level of experience, aptitude, training, and comfort level.

Cover photo by Brian Stevenson

Published by Watercourse LLC

Michael French

In memory of my brother Michael, my rock, my closest friend, and my partner in mischief. He moved through life with a voice of reason and a heart of compassion.

CONTENTS

INTRODUCTION

Author on Ghizar River in Pakistan—photo by Mike Speaks

In the last two decades of the twentieth century as a nascent adventure travel industry found popular appeal, river expeditions offered access to regions rarely traveled. During those wild times, I guided the most renowned whitewater rivers in the world, including the Zambezi, Bio-Bio, Futaleufu, Karnali, Colorado and scores of others.

Anyone who spends hours a day rowing a river will develop a deep relationship with water, often unspoken, almost subliminal. The connection felt between the hands, oars, and river can only be analyzed by logic to a degree, while a deeper communication whispers with mystic undertones.

For thousands of years, the Chinese have contemplated the nuances of water, which embody the essence of Taoism: to yield and overcome. Taoist thought forms the conceptual background of the martial art of Tai Chi, following the principles of yielding to force, sensing imbalance and returning force.

I found that my practice of Tai Chi became integral to my skill in rowing whitewater and the act of rowing whitewater brought me more profound understanding of Taoism, which led me to a deeper awareness of the patterns in flowing water (*li*), the concept of letting go (*wu-wei*) and the inevitability of change (*yin yang*).

My discoveries at the intersection of rowing and Tai Chi have led to this book, which explores the mechanics of rowing whitewater and the spirit of running rivers. This is the book I wish I could have read when I started guiding.

Experienced river guides will feel the ideas hauntingly familiar. Many of these perceptions happen on a molecular level without ever labeling them. It might seem fantastical to the uninitiated, but I hope reading these concepts will expand one's perceptions of rowing whitewater.

PART ONE
READING

1: WHITEWATER SMACKDOWN

Crrytal Rapid, October, 1982—photo by Liz Duckworth

"Failure is the foundation of success, and the means by which it is achieved."

— LAO TZU

I teetered on a tall boulder in the depths of the Grand Canyon, studying Crystal Rapid. A tongue of jade-green water flowed swift and smooth for a hundred yards into a muscular wave that built for twelve seconds before breaking back on itself in a percussive explosion.

Clients dotted the shore with cameras ready. We were running in two groups to give Joe and me a chance to watch the veterans. Joe had been my boss on the South Fork of the American River in California, where I had guided one and two-day trips for the summer. Our route through Crystal would be what they called a cheat run, breaking out of the main current and avoiding the meat of the rapid.

This was my first time rowing such strong currents, big rapids, and giant eddies. The first few days of the trip presented mostly flat water, where the downstream current was often just a thin path between stadium-sized eddies reaching out from both sides of the river.

Each time I got pulled into an eddy, I had to row upstream to break into the current again, throwing me further behind the group. I had tried to mimic Curt, our trip leader, who pushed forward with relaxed strokes, but I couldn't keep up. It seemed like the other rafts were hooked into an invisible underwater tow that I couldn't find. I often had to pull hard to catch up, but rowing backward only drew me into another giant eddy. Now, dropping through the narrow inner gorge of the Canyon, that current had multiplied its power.

I felt I was finally getting a feel for such a big river. I always had an affinity for water from swim teams to body surfing. Maybe I had some magical connection to water that would make me a master river guide. Such were the delusions swirling in my head. Having rowed all the rapids so far without incident, I had convinced myself that I was indeed reading whitewater—much like a third grader looks at a page of Shakespeare and says to himself, "Yeah, I can read that."

Joe stretched high on his boulder and pointed upstream. "Here they come!"

Curt's raft crested the lip of the rapid, stern aimed toward the right shore. His four passengers, still as statues, gripped perimeter ropes, their eyes transfixed by the pounding wave.

Curt looked over his shoulder and rocked back, snapping his oars through the water in a series of powerful strokes.

He was heading straight for a marker rock near the right bank as the current shot his boat downstream. The combination of forces took his raft cleanly past the rock and over the diagonal waves that guarded shore. He slowed his speed and spun his raft into a small eddy.

Cheers erupted for Curt as Liz's raft took the same line. Liz broke through to shore too fast, bounced off a rock, and was almost swept back into the rapid.

Joe and I climbed off the boulders.

I said, "That was slick! One big move and you're golden."

"Timing and momentum, Frenchy."

"You know, it almost looks like you could run that wave if you could hit it when it was building. What a great ride!" I grinned to see if there was any buy-in to my theory.

Joe frowned as he pushed his glasses back up the bridge of his nose. "You don't pull the tail of the tiger."

"Right." I sobered.

"I know you're all focused on that big wave, but look downstream." He pointed to where the river flowed swiftly over a boulder-strewn shoal. "You don't want to get tangled up in that." Of the two channels around the shoal, the left looked fun with lots of waves, while the right channel looked easy and open as it curved around to a large eddy. "You can go left or right, but you have to decide early."

My passengers were standing by the raft, waiting for me when I returned from scouting. Ron, Guy, and Nathan, boatmen from other rivers, had signed on to see the Grand Canyon as helpers.

I hopped on the boat, donned my life jacket, and sat on the commissary boxes that served as my rower's seat. As the trainee, I was rowing the "shit boat," an eighteen-foot raft full of tarps, tents, tables, fire pan, propane tanks, stoves, and eight rocket boxes for taking out every single turd dropped from our group.

While the other rafts had everything stowed neatly away with orderly rows of black rubber bags strapped on the back deck, my boat looked like the sloppy private in the platoon. Odd-shaped items cluttered the raft under a spiderweb of ropes.

"Good luck, Frenchy." Ron, a former bronc rider from Montana, forced a smile as he coiled my bow line and held the raft. Guy and Nathan climbed aboard, wished me luck, and sat on my front deck looking at the shore with the thousand-yard stare of doomed soldiers. There is nothing more difficult for a river guide than riding through a big rapid with a novice like me.

A few yards away, Joe stowed gear and helped his clients tighten their life jackets.

The eleven-foot-long oars felt heavy when I swung their blades out over the water. The bravado I had felt during the scout vanished. I felt a wave of doubt, just shy of panic. Were all the boxes closed? Had I tied everything? Where were my sunglasses? I shipped the oars, stood up in the footwell, and looked around my raft: boxes shut, knots secure, ropes tight. Rigged for a flip, as they say. I sat down, took a swig from my water bottle, and jammed it back into the pile of bags behind me. I discovered my sunglasses hanging around my neck.

Joe signaled he was ready. Ron shoved us off the shore and jumped in with one agile move. I rowed up the eddy to catch the current. "Joe, your life jacket!"

Joe felt his chest and found his life jacket lying behind him. He tucked his oars under his knees and quickly threw on his jacket. I guess Joe had the jitters too. I slid into the current and cautiously pushed toward the middle of the river.

Restless currents boiled and swirled for a hundred yards until they all would come together and barrel into the rapid. Time became a taffy pull between my adrenaline demanding action and the slow flow of the river. I wanted to row, scream, anything except simply float along, keeping my stern aimed to the right shore.

I shook my head and stood up in the footwell, straining to see the rapid. Shoreline tamarisk gave way to hundreds of boulders scattered past the mouth of Crystal Creek. Which one was my marker rock?

The river quickened its slide toward chaos where that monster wave pounded the river, as if calling for my destruction. I couldn't wait any longer. I braced my foot against the frame and rowed while I searched for the marker rock. Finally, I saw it ... further downstream. "Shit!" I dragged my oars in the water. I had started too early. Wait. Patience. I pushed a few strokes back toward the center.

Only a few seconds later, Nathan looked back at me and raised his eyebrows. "I'd start rowing if I were you."

I checked the rock over my shoulder and leaned into a stroke. My riders gripped the ropes and braced themselves. My next pull was stronger and the next almost desperate. For a moment, I thought I'd waited too long. We'd be swept into the wave, flipped, plunged into ice-cold water, and raked through the rocks. Another desperate pull at the oars and the marker rock loomed toward the back of my boat. One more pull and we bashed through the wave below the rock, which sent a chilling flood of water down my neck. PERFECT!

A few strokes through some choppy waves took my raft out of the main current where I swung my bow toward shore and caught a small eddy below Curt's boat.

Humility flipped to hubris in a heartbeat. *I could put the boat where I wanted. I could row!* So much adrenaline coursed through me, dopamine was popping out of my eyes like champagne bubbles. *I was good! I was a prodigy! I needed a victory lap!* I looked at the enticing left channel along the cliff across the river.

With all my reason gripped by temporary madness, I pulled out of the eddy while my riders were bailing and howling with relief. I would cross the river and run the left slot. Never mind that I was on the right shore, and never mind that I couldn't read water worth a damn. I had no idea most of the river was flowing against me, away from where I thought it would be fun to go.

It turns out the left channel was only a contingency if you got sucked into the meat of the rapid and spit out toward the left wall. I did not know that. No. I wrapped up all my hopes and dreams into one big ball of vainglory and rowed back into the rapid.

My gang spun toward me as soon as they felt the boat lurch into the current that we had just escaped. "What are you doing? Where are you going?" They yelled in protest.

"The left side looks like more fun," I shouted with a crazed grin. Their eyes widened.

I rowed as hard as I could to cross the river, but the boat wasn't responding. An invisible wire seemed to be pulling me toward a boulder at the top of the shoal.

"Pull harder!" My riders weren't cheering as much as pleading.

"PULL!"

The oars slapped against waves each time I reached for a stroke. The boat, half full of water, weighed tons. No matter how hard I rowed, my progress slowed. I pulled with all my might.

Someone shouted, "High-side!" Everyone jumped to the downstream side of the boat. It seemed too soon. I still believed that I could make one final stroke, hit the rock with my bow, and spin off the side, but I hit it sideways, dead center of the raft.

We scrambled onto the downstream tube to keep it from sliding up the rock. The raft settled, and we stepped onto the boulder.

Everyone started yelling.

"Push it!"

"Jump on the tube!"

"Thread the bow line through the frame!"

"Get in the boat and pull up the other side!"

We quickly lost the battle. The river overflowed the upstream tube and sucked it under. Game over. No matter what we tried, it only sank deeper. The full power of the Colorado River pounded into bow and stern and splayed my raft across the boulder. Stranded in the middle of the Colorado River, we stood on a rock the size of a picnic table 80 yards from the right shore, and a cliff on the left. In seconds I had gone from boatman to Bozo, prodigy to liability, genius to dunce.

We stood together on that rock like four prisoners. My raft shook and jerked as the river tore into it. Ropes were breaking and bags floating away, each a testament to my blunder.

Joe and Curt launched an empty raft and caught an eddy downstream from us. We threw them a line and pulled his raft up behind our rock. I thought Joe might rip me with some joke, but he was all business. "Everyone okay?"

"Everyone's fine," I said. The others nodded in agreement.

Curt said, "The kayaker went downstream to

retrieve anything floating away. Frenchy, get on the raft, cut away ropes, hand us the gear, and we'll load it into my boat." We were to abandon my raft to the ravages of the river, and any desperate hope I may have held of saving the situation swirled downstream with my sinking heart.

The raft had slipped deeper into the river with only a fraction still out of the water. I tightened my life jacket, slid into the water, and perched on the frame. The river beat at my back and wrapped its icy fingers around my chest.

I moved methodically, one hand or foot at a time. Many of the knots were underwater, and my hands became so numb I had to cut lines rather than untie them. But I had to cut selectively to prevent the whole pile from breaking loose. I worked through the matrix of ropes and bags and boxes and gear, handing them up to the others, carefully, methodically. I had to accept the cold water swirling around me and stay focused, which kept my mind off the disaster I'd created. When I returned to the rock, I was shivering.

A client who was a fishing guide cast a line to us. It was the first time I had ever seen a cast that far, and never from the fish's point of view. After tying thin nylon rope to the fishing line, we signaled Liz on shore, who slowly reeled it back. Holding my breath. I watched the fishing line and white cord snake back to shore. None of us wanted to see that line break. It was a lucky cast, which had taken him a while to hit. When the cord played out, we tied it to a thick static rope, which was hauled ashore, securing the raft.

The river rose, covering my raft entirely, except for the thole pin on the side of the frame. We had to leave the large boxes because it was impossible to lift them out of the frame against the pounding of the river. We piled into Joe's boat and rowed over to Thank God Eddy, the unofficial name of the large eddy below Crystal, also known as ABC for Alive Below Crystal.

I spent the rest of the afternoon lugging gear rescued by the kayaker back to camp from a mile downstream. Each round trip cost me an hour of torturous scrambling across the scree-filled ravines and over diagonal fins of granite, pushing myself mercilessly in a vague yearning for redemption.

As darkness fell, Curt said, "Frenchy, take a break. We'll cook dinner."

I found a secluded spot, laid out my sleeping gear, and collapsed for a few minutes to let my aching muscles rest.

A chain of hot shame hung on me like a rosary of regret. Such a stupid move! No one to blame, but myself. How could we ever get that raft off the rock? What if we didn't get it off? Would we abandon it? Would we need a helicopter to remove it? Would I have to pay? Was this already the end to my guiding career after only three months?

I returned to the kitchen and started helping.

When Curt tried to shoo me away, I said, "I'd rather work than sit around and think."

We cooked burgers and dogs on the lids of bean cans. The commissary boxes remained in the boat, along with all the toilet boxes and supplies. Tables had been lost to the river. Clients donated paperback novels for toilet paper.

That night, Curt slept in a wetsuit next to the kayak. We balanced a bucket of empty beer cans on a rock beside the rope holding the stranded raft. If the boat broke loose, the rope would knock over the bucket of cans, waking Curt, who would kayak out to the raft, yelling to Joe and me, and we would give chase in a raft.

Joe and I bedded down on his raft in the restless eddy that jerked us back and forth against the shore. I slept fitfully to the sound of waves and the roar of Crystal Rapid taunting me in the distance.

———

"Wake up! The boat's off!" The voice of a client named Walter penetrated my sleep.

Joe and I scrambled to our feet and stumbled onto the shore. "What's happening? What time is it?"

Walter spoke quickly. "It's five AM. I had a dream that the boat was off. And look!" The beam from his flashlight swung over the river to where my raft floated in the eddy behind the boulder. That was our first shock. The second was the ghostly figure swaying back and forth in the raft.

"Is that Curt out there?" I asked.

"Looks like Curt's bailing the boat," said Joe.

We picked our way up the rocky shoreline to where Curt had slept. Joe said, "He must've kayaked to the raft."

"Why didn't he yell to us?"

The kayak still sat with its spray-skirt, paddle, helmet, and lifejacket ready to go. The bucket of cans was undisturbed. Next to it all, Curt was sleeping.

"Curt! Wake up! The boat's off!" said Joe.

"What?" Curt mumbled. He rose to his elbow amidst his jumbled sleeping bag, looked at us for a second, and then fumbled for his glasses.

"The wrapped boat is off the rock," Joe yelled as if Curt were hard of hearing.

"We thought you were out there," I added, much to his confusion.

Curt scrambled to his feet and climbed into the kayak. We shoved his kayak into the river, and he paddled into lower Crystal Rapid, which would have been daunting enough in daylight. We followed his progress with our flashlights. The water released from the dam had dropped overnight. If my raft had slid off the far side of the boulder, it might have snagged its rope on the rock and swung into the eddy behind.

We gasped in unison as Curt slipped getting out of the kayak and onto the boulder. He caught himself and carefully lifted the line over the rock and pushed the boat into the current. The rope went taunt and swung the raft toward us. Curt got back into his kayak and nudged the raft along until we could pull it in.

The boat looked like a shipwreck, the frame crooked, commissary askew, boxes upside down, and, most shocking, three of the four outer tubes were deflated. The collapsed raft must have forced the cross tube into the air. So, what had looked like Captain Ahab beckoning to us had actually been the thwart rocking back and forth to the rhythm of the eddy. We de-rigged the damaged raft and pulled it up onto dry cobbles.

At dawn, Liz brought us coffee, which we savored while pondering the stricken boat. Slashes covered the deflated tubes like the victim of a psycho attack.

We laid out rolls of Hypalon, glue, solvents, scissors, sand paper, and brushes on a tarp, and began patching the damage.

Sometime during the first hour, Curt said, "What's this?" He reached through one of the holes and slowly pulled out a kitchen knife. It must have flushed out of the commissary box and plunged into the tube. The force of the water had twirled it around the inside of the tubes, slashing through baffles that separated the chambers, and cutting a dozen holes in the boat.

So my raft had been saved, but the price was high. Throughout it all, Curt took pictures and told me that someday I would be glad I had photos.

Joe, not quite so diplomatic, laughed. "Yeah. Take a lot of pictures, Frenchy. You'll never see this river again!"

That afternoon, with a patched raft and a slightly crooked frame, I floated away from Crystal Rapid. The river served as a balm for my stress, as the challenge of rowing rapids eclipsed thoughts of my blunder.

The night before Lava Falls, anxiety gnawed at my confidence. Guests and guides spun wild tales of terror about Lava Falls, thought to be the fastest navigable rapid in the world. Stories of rafts flipping over and over in the ledge hole, followed by horrible accounts of boats being mangled in the whirlpool next to the Black Rock below the falls, and descriptions of the tail waves as tall as our rafts. I took all those stories to bed with me and did not sleep well.

In the morning, my three passengers from Crystal all volunteered to ride with me again and I felt grateful for their support, albeit a little heavier with responsibility.

For several hours, the river ran peacefully, cradled in silence by stone cliffs, and I found a meditative rhythm in the rowing until the droning rumble of Lava Falls filled the canyon. As we rounded the bend, the dull thundering became the roar of a freight train as the river disappeared over a horizon line.

A mile above Lava Falls, a volcanic core called Vulcan's Anvil towered out of the water like a chipped black obelisk. According to superstition, a small offering would bring good luck in Lava Falls, so I rowed over and tossed a quarter up to the top of the rock. It bounced back into the boat. Rejected! I took off my hat and sunglasses to find the quarter at the bottom of the boat. I stood on the deck to flip the quarter onto a ledge, but it bounced off again and fell in the river. Denied! As I stepped back, I felt the crunch of my mirrored sunglasses under my tennis shoe. I was suddenly feeling very unlucky.

We scouted from rocks high above the rapid. Lava Falls looked enormous and sounded deafening. The river plunged off a ledge, so it would be impossible to see the rapid from a raft until you were cresting the drop, which made the entry point critical. We were attempting the Bubble Line Run. Mysteriously, an occasional upwelling of bubbles in the current led to the lip of the falls at just the right point to skirt the monster ledge hole. Past that, we'd be in position to run a succession of giant waves. Following some bubbles into a blind drop meant committing to a myth. The trick was to center your raft across those bubbles until the last second and then pivot the bow downstream.

After twenty minutes of staring down at miles of streaking current, I raised my eyes toward the cliffs across from us and they seemed to be melting. I had never had an acid flashback, but imagined this was what it would look like. I asked Joe about it and he assured me the cliffs weren't melting. "Just look away from the rapid occasionally."

When Curt and Liz ran the rapid, their eighteen-foot rafts disappeared in the crashing waves and emerged brimming with water. Curt eddied out behind the Black Rock, tied his raft, and climbed back up to the scout rock. Liz waited in her raft downstream. Curt would direct me onto the bubble line from the cliff. It was remedial aid for novice boaters, but Curt wanted no more mishaps.

I tried to keep my mind focused as I walked back to the boats. My heart was pounding the bass rhythm to a Greek chorus of doubts in my head.

I rowed away from shore and saw Curt standing on the rocks high above the river. I straddled the current, ready to pull or push toward the bubbles. I couldn't see anything beyond the horizon line, so I concentrated on Curt.

As I approached the horizon line, Curt waved me toward the opposite shore. I gently pulled back. The current seemed so soft here. I could see the bubbles were going under the back of my raft, but I wasn't quite on top of them. Curt waved again to the left shore. I pulled a little harder. Damn! The bubbles were still under my stern. The current was quickening and my anxiety peaking. Curt again waved me toward the left. In my frustration, I gave two hard pulls. Now the raft responded with enthusiasm and shot past the bubbles.

My riders turned to me in horror and for the second time that trip they shouted, "Where are you going?"

I was backing dead sideways toward the center of the largest hole on the river. The bubble line was gone, and we were a second from launching over the edge of the cataclysm.

"Straighten it out!" everyone shouted in chorus as they held tight.

I spun the bow to the lip of the falls and looked down into a relentless, breaking wave big enough to swallow three rafts. We dropped over the ledge into a wall of water. I expected to be stopped, spun, flipped, and punished, but, as if cradled by a benign hand, we passed through the crush of water and blasted sideways into a towering wave train. I struggled to turn the boat, brimming with water, to face the waves, but I couldn't get it around and the next wave smacked the raft sideways. I yelled, "High-side!" I let go of the oars and gripped the thole pin like a saddle horn.

We were in survival mode, holding onto the side of the raft like a bucking bronco as waves shot us skyward. When the wave train finished with us, we spun on the current below the rapid. I quickly fished my oars out of the water, slid them onto their pins, and caught the eddy below a freshwater spring. When we hit the beach, we all started laughing. I was in stitches. I was laughing so hard I couldn't speak, but I finally croaked, "It really is better to be lucky than good."

The other boats slid into the eddy, and we bailed the rafts and regaled each other.

Joe shouted, "Hey, Mister Excitement!"

Curt laughed and said, "I thought you were going to flip for sure. I told the clients to get their cameras ready."

Liz said, "Don't listen to them, Frenchy. Any run through Lava right-side-up is a good run."

News travels fast in the Grand Canyon. By the time we pulled into Diamond Creek, everyone had heard about my wrap at Crystal. Mike Walker, the area manager, slapped me on the back and said, "You're an expensive trainee, Frenchy." Although he said it with a smile, I figured it might be a long time before I ever got to row the Colorado River through the Grand Canyon again.

On the drive back to Flagstaff, Curt showed me his trip report. The report noted I had not lost composure in the Crystal Rapid incident and no one had been injured. It emphasized how hard I worked and said I could row well enough, but I needed greater skill at reading water.

My bubble had burst. I was not a rowing prodigy.

Evidently, anyone could learn to row, but good kitchen help was hard to find.

It was the end of the rafting season, a time to put things away, but my blunder at Crystal stuck in my gut. In November, I lay on a beach in Mexico and looked across an azure sea at an abandoned, rusting freighter that tilted in the shallows between islands. It loomed large in the small channel and I felt it towered above my blunder. I guess they couldn't read water either! What a humiliating memorial. It gave me hope that there were no such monuments to my embarrassment.

When I returned from Mexico, I called Mike Walker and convinced him to schedule me on the first trip of the season, starting on April 15. I didn't calculate it at the time, but that meant I would row Crystal Rapid on my thirty-third birthday.

2: READING WATER, AN ANALYSIS

Author scouting the Zambezi—photo by Jib Ellison

"The art of life is more like navigation than warfare, for what is important is to understand the winds, the tides, the currents, the seasons, and the principles of growth and decay, so that one's actions may use them and not fight them."

— ALAN WATTS

At the OARS Whitewater Guide School, we learned the basics of river guide work: captaining a paddle raft, rowing an oar boat, river rescues, cooking, camping, boat repair, and navigating rapids. The one skill they couldn't teach was how to read water, but they tried.

One morning, our instructor, who everyone called Captain Kirk, grew irritated with how we commanded our paddle raft as if it had an outboard motor, zigzagging about the river and wearing everyone out. He took the captain's position and aimed us toward a small waterfall just inches wider than our raft.

"Forward paddle, one stroke." We complied, and with that small momentum, the raft scooted toward the rocks framing the slot.

"Right turn, one stroke." He deftly drew the boat around and we slipped through the drop without touching the rocks.

We looked at him in awe. Kirk said, "The river will take you downstream. You just have to get on the piece of it going your way."

Indeed. Just get on the piece of it going your way. But how do you determine which piece? That is the art of reading water.

RIVER FEATURES

Some things just cannot fit into the narrow confine of words. River runners have named all the features you will ever find on a rapid, but reading water is better understood through experience rather than explanation. Recognizing features is just the beginning. You must also know what those features would do to the type of boat you have and how much power they have at different flows. There are many illustrations of these features available, but it is better to observe them in a river to understand how to use their motion and when to avoid them.

The perspective looking downstream is always used to describe anything on a river. The sides of the river are referred to as river-left or river-right from the upstream viewpoint, looking downstream.

Here are the principal features of moving water in a rapid and how to read them:

Pillow Wave: The current hits an exposed boulder and bounces back. Look for a rock being buffered on the upstream side by a cresting wave.

Undercut: When a significant amount of water piles into a rock or cliff but does not form a pillow wave, it may flush down into an undercut. This is extremely dangerous.

Pour-over: When the river spills over a rock or ledge, it creates a small waterfall. Pour-overs create strong upstream flow in the reversal on the downstream side. Look for water pouring vertically over the back of an obstacle. From upstream, it may only appear as a slight hump in the river.

Hole: As more water flows over an obstacle, it

creates a circular backflow. Look for a depression with a wave that constantly breaks upstream. Holes often have a frothy, turbulent appearance. Holes can suck in surrounding current.

Keeper Hole: Both pour-overs and holes can be difficult to exit against all the water recycling upstream. If you are stuck in a hole, the quickest way for a swimmer to escape is to go deep and get flushed out along the bottom, because the surface water just churns back into the hole.

Frowning Hole: When the edges of a hole curl upstream like a frown, it allows no exit from the edges of the hole and creates a stronger keeper.

Smiling Hole: When the edges curl downstream in a smile, the hole releases water downstream from its edges. Maneuver to an edge of the hole to catch downstream current. Most holes have this shape.

Ledge Hole: A low head dam forms a perfect recycle of water, allowing no escape on the surface. The more a hole is perfectly straight across and square to the current, the more deadly it becomes.

Flushing Hole: If a portion of the recycling flow flushes downstream, it often looks like a plume of water flowing downstream through the break. This is what to aim for when running a hole.

Wave: More water over that same obstacle creates a rise in the water's surface to fill the void and smooth the trough to create a *wave*.

Standing Wave: Typically, standing waves are tall, smooth and predictable.

Breaking Wave: A standing wave occasionally curls over and breaks upstream on itself like an ocean wave. The difference between a breaking wave and a hole is its elevation and how often it breaks. A hole will be constantly breaking.

Rooster Tail: A standing wave that peels off both sides rather than breaking back upstream.

Eddy: The river will flow around any feature in its path to create an eddy. The eddy current flows upstream to fill in the void left by the obstruction. The shoreline impedes the current and creates eddies at every intrusion into the river. Look for areas of relatively calm water behind obstacles where the current flows upstream.

Eddy Line, Eddy Wall: Eddies are often marked by a foam line where the upstream flow meets the downstream current. The line between those opposing currents is the eddy line and, when fast enough, can create a ridge or wall between them. The eddy line is narrow at the top of the eddy (furthest upstream section) and widens at the bottom of the eddy. When trying to catch an eddy, enter as high on the eddy line as possible. In high water, an eddy line wall will be its tallest at the top of the eddy. Boils and whirlpools can appear at the top of eddies, their size depending on the speed of the current.

Whirlpool: When opposing currents brush shoulders violently, they swing around in a whirlpool.

Boil: An upwelling of water caused by strong currents below the surface. When the river bounces up from a boulder in the riverbed, it pushes a convex mound to the surface. This often happens in flood stage and sometimes at the top of an eddy. Look for a hump of water boiling up.

V-Waves: When there is a constriction in the river, it shoves the river into a narrow channel. Opposing lateral waves come together to create a single or a series of triangular shaped waves.

Wave Train: A series of waves lined up one after the other.

Tongue: Smooth, V-shaped flow of water indicates the main current through a rapid. The current running down the center of the river gets squeezed ever narrower between diagonal waves and looks like a giant tongue leading into the heart of the rapid. The V-shaped path of smooth water pointing downstream is usually the deepest, fastest part of the rapid.

Upstream V: A small eddy line appears as a foamy V pointing upriver, revealing the tip of a slightly submerged obstruction.

River Bend: The deepest channel and fastest water sweeps to the outside of a curve. Stay to the inside for caution unless you know the route well. If you go in the fast outside channel, take an angle that will keep you from running into the outside bank.

Cut Bank: As the river erodes a bank over time, it cuts into the land and leaves a vertical face.

Shoal: A sand, cobble, or gravel bar that gathers into a shallow section of the river. It often has many small waves at its location, usually with a deeper channel running beside it.

Strainer: Obstacles like fallen trees that allow water to pass through, can trap boats or swimmers. These obstacles are commonly located where the banks have eroded, particularly on the outside of river bends. It's very difficult to break free of a strainer. If you float toward one and can't get away, swim toward it with your legs stretched on the surface behind you. Grab it and launch yourself on top of it. If the strainer sweeps your legs below it, you will never be able to get on top by yourself. Strainers are deadly. Avoid areas where water flows through or under obstructions.

Sieve: Like a strainer but with rocks. This can entrap a swimmer. Avoid at all costs.

Turbulent flow: A swimmer in the water will move downstream faster than the raft, because they are catching more of the current. If your boat flips and you are upstream of it, you have only moments to grab a line or launch yourself on top before the current sweeps you under the raft.

All these features combine in an infinite number of ways to create rapids. Each feature can be powerful or harmless depending on two other major factors: river gradient, measured in feet per mile; and volume which is measured in cubic feet per second (cfs).

Think of all the language built from twenty-six letters in the alphabet, or the music created from a scale of twelve notes and seven octaves. Out of the infinite possibilities, each rapid and every river combines elements and features in a unique expression of its spirit. It is not enough to just recognize the features. You must gauge each challenge on the day you meet it.

WHITEWATER CLASSIFICATIONS

- Class I - Current
- Class II - Riffles
- Class III - Rapid
- Class IV - Difficult rapid
- Class V - Dangerous rapid
- Class VI - Death

SCOUTING

A river never stands still. Fortunately, the features of a rapid that pulse with surges of strength don't change their position in a river. So the easiest way to identify river features is from shore when scouting a rapid. Start from the bottom of the rapid and work your way up to assess where you want to go and how to get there.

Considerations when scouting:

- How do volume, gradient, speed, and direction interact and influence each other to create the rapid?
- Observe the river's flow, direction and speed. Many currents make up a rapid and not all flow downstream.
- Estimating distance and time available to navigate between waves, holes, and eddies is essential for picking a route.
- Where could you catch an eddy?
- Where do the holes or waves you might run flush through the most?
- Which current goes where you want to be? Can you ride that into position?
- Do you need momentum at the entry?
- If you are entering stern-first for momentum, where can you spin forward?
- How can you use the features to aid your run instead of fighting them?
- What are key markers you can recognize from river level?

READ AND RUN

A rapid might look clearly laid out from the scout rock and completely different from the river. That is why you must look at a rapid again, as close to river level as possible after scouting to identify your markers.

Most of the time, you won't be scouting rapids, but just reading as you run. You may have a map to consult or someone to follow who knows the way, but, when you arrive above that rapid, you have to read the features and act quickly.

Features can be tough to differentiate from the water level above a rapid, especially when the river is steep. Sometimes it just seems like a massive confusion of frothy water. Where's the main current? Are there obstructions? Is that hump of white a pour-over or hole? Does it flush? All these questions must be answered in a flash. It is often too much for mere intellect to grasp as quickly as needed. Fortunately, the mind has a skill called pattern recognition.

PATTERN RECOGNITION

> "The labyrinth of the nervous system can integrate more variables than the scanning process of conscious attention."
>
> — ALAN WATTS

Pattern recognition is like viewing an abstract painting that depicts patterns and color rather than individual elements. It's the pattern that speaks to your subconscious.

Rapid visual pattern recognition in whitewater involves a highly coordinated effort across multiple brain regions and processes. By processing visual information, detecting features, integrating memory, focusing attention, making predictions, and coordinating responses, the brain allows for quick and effective recognition of patterns.

The detection of recurring visual elements is essential in whitewater for identifying specific water conditions. The ability to recognize whitewater features depends heavily on experience. Seasoned guides develop an intuitive understanding of how to read water by building a mental catalog of visual patterns associated with different river conditions.

There is more going on than mere intellectual analysis. Pattern recognition is a golden skill that elevates any athlete in a fast-paced sport. That especially applies to running whitewater.

PRACTICAL TRAINING

To build that storehouse of pattern recognition, you must view rivers with an eye to identifying patterns. The more you reinforce that recognition, the more quickly you will be able to retrieve it. Here are some of the best ways to learn about rapids from the best teacher of all, the river itself:

- Scout rapids and ask what more experienced guides are seeing.
- Toss a stick to where you want to enter the rapid and see where it ends up.
- Watch others run rapids and see what they do, what works, and what doesn't.
- Run the same river at different levels.
- Run as many rivers as possible.
- Ride along with an experienced guide. What do they see? How do they row it?
- When you gain more confidence, row lead boat so you can't follow others.
- Run different watercraft, especially a kayak if you can.
- Gradually increase the difficulty of the rivers you run.
- Analyze recordings of runs through rapids.
- Test what you know.
- Find confidence in what you know.

MENTAL TRAINING

"To clarify muddy waters, you must hold them still and let things settle. To glimpse the secret of the Tao, you must keep still and quiet your mind."

— LAO TSU, *TAO TE CHING*

Meditation can improve focus and concentration, enhancing the ability to quickly recognize visual patterns. There are many resources for learning to meditate; all share the goal of calming the mind and letting go of intellectual thoughts. Some simple techniques include breathing techniques and mantras.

Mindfulness practice in everyday life develops situational awareness to stay attentive to your physical surroundings. If you need a good example of this, watch a server with a full tray of glasses navigate a crowded bar. They will be attentive to the movements of every person around them as they slide through the gaps.

Play pattern recognition games like puzzles, chess, checkers, or Go.

Reading water is a critical skill for river runners, but trying to explain how to read water is like diagramming how to dance. River features have to be ingrained in your mind, so you can recognize them at a glance. Study, while useful for basics, will not further your ability to read water as well as direct experience. Any encounter with moving water, from a rivulet to a flood, can offer lessons.

Reading water can be fascinating. Not reading water can be deadly, as I discovered during my second year of guiding.

3: DEADLY CONSEQUENCES

Crystal Rapid, 1983—photo by Curt Smith

"The only thing more dangerous than ignorance is arrogance."

— ALBERT EISTEIN

S now blanketed Flagstaff when I arrived in mid-April to resurrect my reputation in the Grand Canyon. The area manager said I would be rowing alongside two of the best guides in the world. Jim Slade, the senior guide for Sobek Expeditions, had racked up more first descents of wild rivers around the world than any other human. With Hollywood good looks and a shock of brown hair that fell to one side, he spoke with authority and precision. Tony Anderson, a top Canyon guide for OARS, was a bulldozer of a man with dark brown hair, a muscular physique, a handlebar mustache, and eyes like big blue saucers of mischief.

The river was running high at over 20,000 cfs. As the first commercial trip of the season, we had no reports of what lay ahead. Tony took me under his wing and taught me exactly how he wanted everything done: how to run the kitchen, secure the rafts, set up a porta-potty, and the etiquette of living on your raft.

On the fifth day, we descended into the wild rapids of the Granite Gorge where sheer cliffs made scouting problematic. I could tell by the timbre of their voices and the way they meticulously rigged their rafts that morning, Tony and Jim were jacked to be running big rapids in high water.

Tony said, "I want Jim on my tail, but stay close behind us."

They ran the meat of everything, while I cheated

some rapids by rowing along the edge of danger. A few times, they sent me ahead to provide safety for their daring runs. We all ran Crystal Rapid without incident, unaware that years would pass before Crystal would ever be that easy again.

At Bass Camp, yellow blossoms of brittlebush covered the hills. With Crystal behind me, the bloom of desert spring inspired me to look around and loosen my focus from the challenges of the river. While Jim prepared dinner, Tony took me on a scramble to the ridge above Shinumo Canyon. A storm cloud broke as we toasted our successful runs and my birthday with whiskey, laughing at the rain and shouting into the thunder. Tony suggested I row a baggage boat on his Hiker's Special trip in October. That was what I had wanted—to resurrect my reputation and get more chances to train as a Grand Canyon guide.

CALIFORNIA CARNAGE

In mid-May, I returned to the American River. A record-setting snowpack loomed in the mountains across the west. Rivers were running high, swift, and cold.

While guiding a paddle raft with a crew of friends, I experienced my first flip at Troublemaker Rapid. We righted the raft and paddled on, full of adrenaline-fueled laughter.

That was the first year river photographers started

filming the main rapids on the South Fork. So many novice guides and boaters on a suddenly dangerous river created some exciting footage. Every afternoon, a pizza joint would screen the dramas of the day with rafts flipping and swimmers scrambling for safety. Some howled with laughter and some of us cringed in horror as a raft shot through the air and landed on top of another raft full of paddlers stuck in a hole.

It was getting so wild, some called for a halt to raft trips on Memorial Day weekend, when every guide and raft available would be on the water. At our guide house, Joe moderated a heated discussion about canceling trips. The river was spilling its banks and making rapids unrecognizable. Half the guides thought it was too wild to navigate safely, while many of us were eager to run it.

No company canceled trips. That weekend dozens of rafts filled the eddy above the first rapid, named Meatgrinder because of its rock-filled structure. All those rocks had become sharp holes and explosive waves. As my crew paddled into the wave train along the right shore, I saw rafts strewn about the rapid, many upside down. The raft in front of us flipped, and we veered right.

As our raft spun out of the bottom of the rapid, we pulled in as many swimmers as we could catch. I looked up and froze. A few feet away on a ledge, guides were performing CPR on a blue-faced man in a wetsuit. We were busy rescuing our own as the river spirited us downstream and the scene disappeared like the flash of nightmare. It turned out the blue-faced man had died from a ruptured heart vessel that no amount of CPR could have helped.

But tragedy was no competition to our lust for adrenaline. OARS started offering trips on the Middle Fork of the American River, and Joe assigned me with three other guides to run those trips. On weekends, we escaped the circus atmosphere of the South Fork and ran a quasi-wilderness two-day river trip. I led many of them. I could be lazy when following others, but suddenly others were following me. That responsibility sharpened my attention on reading the river.

GRAND CANYON IN FLOOD

In June I returned to Arizona. Paramount Pictures had chartered a Grand Canyon trip for executives and directors. OARS added an extra raft to carry enough ice for their cocktails and I got my third training trip.

A record snowpack of the western basin was descending into Lake Powell behind Glen Canyon Dam, fifteen miles upstream from our put-in at Lee's Ferry. The dam was releasing over 40,000 cfs, twice as much as I had run in April.

No one who boated through the Grand Canyon in late June 1983 will ever forget their trip. The power of the river strained the bounds of hyperbole. I didn't know how to process what was happening, but I took my clues from the other guides who were veterans of the Colorado River. Their hardened attitudes seemed humbled by what we were encountering.

The rapids we normally feared were gone or gentled by so much flow, but the river raged and bashed at the shoreline, creating eddy line walls higher than the rafts. Whirlpools appeared out of nowhere and traveled around the river as if hunting for a victim. Once caught, we could only hang on for the ride and hope it didn't flip the raft. Rafting that high water was like riding an endlessly powerful serpentine beast in a discordant dance with all the river's elements.

I watched how guides timed their strokes to match the waves, where they would break into eddies, and how aggressively they challenged big whitewater. But mimicking such good rowers got me in trouble, as I didn't always understand their intent.

Big Bruce, the trip leader, was a master oarsman. At six foot seven inches and two hundred sixty pounds, his orange life jacket looked like a postage stamp on his back. On the third afternoon, he signaled to eddy-out below President Harding Rapid.

As others pulled hard and early for the eddy, I followed Bruce, who floated toward the center of the river. Normally, a giant boulder split the river in two, but instead of a towering boulder, a massive pillow wave broke off the almost submerged rock. Bruce floated dangerously close to it. At the last second, with a giant sweep of his oars, he surfed his raft back off the pillow and rode the trailing lateral wave a hundred yards to the eddy below.

Panic struck me with the feeling I had neither the skill nor strength for such a maneuver, and I frantically pulled for the eddy to avoid that rock and its wave. It took all my strength to make it with such a late start. Once safely in the eddy, I slumped over my oars and croaked to myself, "New rule: never follow Big Bruce!" In years to come, I would understand that Bruce was simply making use of what the river offered him. His insight and skill made that move so sweet.

———

To everyone's amazement, the river rose by the hour. We didn't know what we would find in the deepest part of the canyon, where the biggest run of rapids awaited. Into the gorge we descended. Its black walls swallowed our little bobbing rafts along a chocolate-brown highway. The river flowed over the rapids with ease but slammed into walls with surprising vengeance. After an easy run at Horn Creek, we cheated Granite and floated through Hermit with ease.

Crystal Rapid had only been a minor riffle until 1966, when a monumental winter flood flashed through Crystal Creek, bulldozing sediment and boulders into the river. This happened after the construction of Glen Canyon Dam, so the Colorado River had never scoured Crystal Rapid with its seasonal floods. Crystal was still a young rapid with a wealth of boulders choking it and now the Colorado had risen to become more powerful than any time since the dam.

It was almost noon when we arrived at Crystal. The little beach where we normally stopped was underwater, so we nudged into the hillside, tied off and hiked up to an overview, where we could see a massive breaking wave swallowing most of the river. The rapid thundered, and the earth shook. We could hear boulders rolling and colliding in the river. The river was reconfiguring the rapid right before our eyes, conjuring a giant hole that sucked everything into it, except for a narrow ribbon of swirling water along the right shore. Exclamations of awe came from under each guide's breath.

Tamarisk trees that normally marked the shoreline stood out in the river, bent from the wind off the rapid and waved their skinny leaves as if in fear. We decided to walk our passengers around the rapid, and row empty boats over the tamarisks and along the shoreline. The paddleboat captain said his crew would portage. They argued about it for a minute, but he held firm that although it looked possible, the risk outweighed the reward, and there was plenty more whitewater ahead.

With grim faces, we each shoved off and rowed into the swirling brown water. I couldn't see the rapid as I floated toward it, but once it appeared I could only glance at the monster hole in fear that it would mesmerize me into missing a stroke. I pulled as if my life depended on it and the right channel proved wide enough to skirt the rapid. We all made it without incident and had lunch on the beach where we had patched my raft the previous year. After that, running a series of rapids named after gemstones was pure joy, a dance with big waves under a blazing sun.

We scouted the approach to Bass Camp's harbor, which was guarded by a giant fin of granite and schist that normally stood several feet high. That wall of rock, now submerged, pushed the main current away from the camp in a great flush of boils and whirlpools. If anyone missed the eddy, we would have to row further to search for a camp out of slim pickings downstream.

Bruce went first. If he couldn't make it, we didn't need to try. Of course he made it, but it didn't look easy. He tied up his raft and stationed himself at the bottom of the rapid with throw ropes. I went next because if I could make it, they figured, anyone could, and if I missed it, nobody else had to try.

I needed a big head of steam and some powerful rowing to break that boiling eddy line. With the stern pointed toward camp, I started rowing like hell. At first, I made progress, but soon the persistent roiling water slowed the raft and pushed me back toward the center of the river. It was going to be close. My swamper, Patti, was in the bow watching shore. "Row! Harder! You can do it!"

My arms were shaking, my hands cramping, my back spasming, and the boat felt like it was dragging an anchor.

"Don't give up!" With that, she jumped to the back of the boat to catch the rope from Bruce. "You're getting it." My strokes caught purchase, and the raft slid into the very bottom of the eddy. We hauled our raft further up the shore, and we tied off in the trees where we normally set the kitchen. Everyone made it with a great deal of effort. Of all the things that I did that trip, making the pull into Bass eddy was my proudest accomplishment.

In the heat of the afternoon, a Park Service helicopter swooped past and dropped a note in a Ziplock bag of sand tied with a ribbon. It read, "Glen Canyon Dam released 65,000 cfs this a.m. Should reach you in about seven hours. Camp high, stay safe. The Park Service."

We looked at each other and said, "Higher?" After that, speculation ran rampant about what to do if Glen Canyon Dam broke and sent a wall of water roaring down on us.

Some guides said they would jump in a raft and cut it loose. "Go for the wild ride, because you are probably fucked anyway."

Others thought they could quickly scamper high.

High enough? Quick enough? I started studying routes up from every camp. It wasn't very comforting. Sleeping on the boats became fraught with dreams of being swept downstream in the night.

Our greatest rowing challenge came from a normally calm section before Deer Creek. Fins of rock jutted into the river from one side then the other like great baffles that pinched the river into a narrow slot. The river sloshed through that squeeze in a riot of boils, bubbles, whirlpools, all while shooting the raft toward the wall like a paper airplane. I dug in to pull back, but there was so much froth and bubbles the oars had little purchase. I double-timed my strokes, a windmill of strain, and missed the wall by inches. Below there we rowed right into the pool below Deer Creek Falls and sat in the cooling spray. We were blithely rowing into spaces where we would normally need to hike.

Signs of catastrophe soon caught up with us. At first, it was an abundance of beers floating downstream. An unwritten river rule dictates that any beer captured from the river should be consumed on the spot, but we couldn't possibly drink all we were capturing. Soon we saw river bags and metal boxes floating by, a sure sign of a major mishap upstream. Our discussions of what to do in a great flood took a more serious tone as the river continued to rise.

Lava Falls offered an easy route down the left side,

and we finished the trip without incident. At take out, we learned the Park Service had closed the river after a motor rig had flipped in Crystal Rapid. Even though the river had risen to over 90,000 cfs, I couldn't imagine what size wave could flip a raft as big as two Greyhound buses lashed together.

As more information became public over the years, it became clear how close we had come to a catastrophic flood that would have killed us all. As far as scrambling to high ground, an engineering study stated that if the dam failed, downstream safety could only be reached by ascending the equivalent of a forty-story building. And the fantasy of riding the wave was equally ridiculous as the river would have been a meat grinder of trees and debris, which would have wiped out all the bridges and infrastructure in the Canyon.

Quick work and engineering with the improvised addition of plywood boards along the rim was all that prevented the overtopping of Glen Canyon Dam. Plywood boards! And it was not an overabundance of caution. They erected the barrier overnight, and the reservoir soon rose within inches from the top of the boards. Meanwhile, the spillway tunnels were cavitating and spitting out car-sized chucks of cement in the plume of release.

Crystal Rapid took its place in the history books of

the Grand Canyon when it produced a thirty-foot breaking wave. The unprepared paid the price with lives and injuries, but it was not the little oar boats that suffered. It was the big unwieldy motorized rafts, thirty-six-foot-long rubber barges with dozens of passengers, that believed they would never flip. They didn't scout Crystal and either couldn't read the river or couldn't cut out of the rapid in time to catch the narrow ribbon of safety along the shore. Their raft flipped in the hole, which tore the pontoons apart, slamming metal boxes and frameworks on those caught under the boat. All were swept downstream. Crews of smaller rafts gathered survivors from eddies and cliffs while the Park Service scrambled helicopters to coordinate rescue.

Three people lost their lives, and many sustained injuries. Most of the other big rafts cut out of the rapid in time. By reading the river, they directed their boats against the current, accelerated the engine, and bumped along the shoreline.

LESSONS FROM KAYAKING

When I returned to the American River, I resurrected an old kayak that had been growing weeds by a guide house. A kayak is like the motorcycle of the river, responding to every nuance of current. A paddle raft is like a sports car, because you can move it in any direction, even sideways. While an oar raft is like a bus, filled with baggage and passengers, hard to get moving and hard to stop, with limited options for maneuvers.

Every day after work, I paddled that old kayak out to a riffle below our guide house. To surf the wave created by old bridge pilings, I learned to focus on what was happening directly in front of my boat and ride the current rushing under my boat straight on. Any variance to my angle would wash me off the wave.

To break out of the top of the eddy onto the wave, I had to find a perfect angle. With too little angle, I would struggle directly against the current. With too much, the current would push me sideways and wash me downstream. But with a forty-five-degree angle, I floated onto the wave effortlessly.

Paddling so close to the water let me feel like a river creature. It felt fun, challenging and free spirited, but no one was going to pay me to kayak, so I translated that feel for currents to my rafting maneuvers.

Rivers ran full all summer and whenever we had a few days off, a gang of us ran the Tuolumne River, a beautiful wilderness river filled with rapids. It was called a technical river because many of the rapids required multiple maneuvers. We traded off captaining the rafts and I got to see other techniques and viewpoints. Pushing my skills incrementally on such a challenging river soon made the American River seem easy.

SURVIVOR'S GUILT

When I arrived at the Flagstaff warehouse in October with a small pack of clothes, Tony asked if that was the only pack I had.

He said, "This is called the Hiker's Special for a reason. We'll be hiking far up some side canyons to camp, and you'll be our sherpa! Grab that big frame-pack from the back of the warehouse."

The river had receded, but was still flowing over 45,000 cfs, perfect for getting downriver quickly to hike more trails in the cool fall weather. Tony and his good friend, Lester, would row the clients. My swamper was a river guide, who I will call Jordan.

Our clients were eight women, Girl Scout leaders from Chicago, a sweet group of older, slow hikers. This was a good thing for me, because Tony expected me to lead many of the hikes, while he and Lester went on radical explorations farther than any trails.

At Nankoweep, I loaded that big pack with all the pots and pans and food it could carry. After a few hours of hiking up the canyon, I unloaded everything at our camp under some cottonwood trees. Tony and Lester looked at me with grave disappointment in their eyes. "Where's the beer?"

I hoisted the empty pack on my back, "I'll be right back." I trotted back to the boats to retrieve a full case of beer.

Those efforts were worth it. Tony and Lester filled

me with their knowledge of the Canyon and shared secrets discovered over the years. I even got pulled into their games when they would ambush one another as if they were in an old Western novel. I might be ambling through some bushes in the dark only to hear Lester mumble from the shadows, "If I were an Indian, you'd be dead."

My swamper was visibly upset each time we scouted a big rapid. At Crystal Rapid, Jordan stood apart with arms crossed as we scouted. The colossal hole had settled down to only monstrous. The new challenge was a snapping diagonal wave off the shore that stood six feet high. If the raft couldn't break through that wave, it would slingshot straight into the hole. I noticed Jordan's hands trembled while stowing the rope, but we made it through with a big momentum breakout squarely over that diagonal wave.

When we scouted a thundering Lava Falls, Jordan retreated to the rafts after one glance and was pacing nervously when I returned. We had no problem running left instead of the tricky right side.

On our last night in camp, Jordan drank heavily and confided in me that a fellow guide had drowned when their raft flipped in a keeper. The rescue had been terrifying and CPR useless. Survivor's guilt overwhelmed Jordan.

The intensity of Jordan's grief combined with the deaths I had encountered that year made me reevaluate guiding whitewater. How would I respond in such a crisis? If someone died in my arms, how would I handle it?

Rafting could be deadly. It seemed the underlying reason for accidents involved either a lack of respect for the river's power, or insufficient understanding of its hydrology. Failing to read water accurately could prove deadly.

CHAPTER 4
4: CONFIDENCE

Author on Cal Salmon River, 1985—W.O.A. Photography

"To stick your hands into the river is to feel the cords that bind the earth together in one piece."

— BARRY LOPEZ

Woefully unprepared to handle injuries and deaths like those in my second season, that winter I trained as an EMT (Emergency Medical Technician) along with San Francisco firefighters and future paramedics. Wilderness First Responder courses were not in existence, so I became the guy with all the conditional questions about what could be done when you had no hospital or oxygen available. The teacher, displaying remarkable tolerance, instructed me on what was achievable and the legal boundaries.

I spent my evening hours playing the ancient Chinese game of Go with a friend who brought the board while I supplied the sake. One by one, we placed our respective black or white stones on a grid etched on a wooden board, trying to encircle each other's stones.

Early in a game, I would think of each placement and the consequences like a chess match. As the board filled with stones and my stomach filled with sake, my viewpoint shifted and the stones flowed in shapes. Instead of small skirmishes, the overall dynamic between the stones revealed itself in the patterns of black and white.

I realized that reading water was like reading those stones. You can't analyze it into submission. Sometimes, an unfocused gaze reveals the patterns the intellect does not recognize, because the subconscious can more quickly recognize patterns than the thinking mind.

The Taoist concept of *li* contemplates patterns in nature. In *Tao: The Watercourse Way*, Alan Watts, described *li* as "the asymmetrical, nonrepetitive, and unregimented order which we find in the patterns of moving water, the forms of trees and clouds, of frost crystals on the window, or the scattering of pebbles on beach sand."

When searching for a route through whitewater, guides assess all the patterns in the river's flow to find their line, or optimal route. You can often navigate whitewater with little effort by following a line that flows with the patterns, or *li*. It is the line of greatest ease, from breaking over a wave at the softest spot, to riding a wave train straight down the center, or cutting into an eddy gracefully.

By tapping into both the conscious and subconscious, you can detect features consciously, while utilizing your intuition to navigate with the natural patterns. Even when a route cuts across the grain, it should account for the angle of flow and use it to aid the move. For example, use a forty-five-degree angle to surf across the current, or recognize a soft eddy line to help spin the raft, or ride the rail of a lateral wave into position, or pivot at the top of the wave when the raft is weightless. This approach can change a run from simply rowing away from each danger to dancing with the river and using its features.

Confidence is not gained easily, but builds gradually as one goes from ignorance to knowledge through a series of challenging experiences. Only by experiencing failure and success can one truly secure confidence.

In the spring of my third season, I guided on the Cal Salmon, one of the most technical rivers commercially run in Northern California. It pushed me to my limits. Rapids came fast and furious and I had to trust my instincts second by second. After that, the Tuolumne River did not seem so daunting.

Curt Smith, who had been a mentor to me since guide school and the trip leader on my disastrous first Canyon trip, encouraged me to request a guide spot on the Zambezi River in Africa. Although I felt I didn't have enough experience, I signed up. What the hell. Fake it till you make it.

The Zambezi River flows east across the southern half of Africa from Congo to Mozambique. When it crosses between Zambia and Zimbabwe, it plunges three hundred feet into the first of seven narrow gorges that slash back and forth across the basalt plateau like lightning bolts. The falls thunder and the ground shakes as mist billows into the sky, imparting its name, Mosi-oa-Tunya, or The Smoke that Thunders. The British named it Victoria Falls.

No one had ever navigated the gorge until 1981,

when Sobek Expeditions ran the first descent below the falls, shortly after the Rhodesian Bush War. In five days, Sobek's finest guides incurred multiple croc attacks, flipped five rafts and evacuated one paddler with broken ribs, along with their star TV personality, who abandoned the project. Sobek decided that the post-war return of tourists to Victoria Falls would make the Zambezi a stellar attraction, if they could find guides crazy enough to row it.

When I finally made it into the exclusive Sobek international river guide team, the opportunity wasn't as fabulous as it seemed. No senior Sobek guide wanted to take the daily beating the Zambezi dished out in its powerful rapids, the threat of crocodiles, or the malaise of malaria—all for five dollars a day and sixty kwacha, which was worthless outside of Zambia. I paid nine hundred dollars for my airfare over and hoped to make enough kwacha to buy a ticket home. But none of that mattered. I was there to run some big whitewater and prove myself to Sobek. That's what we all came for.

The Zambezi one-day trip had ten rapids, seven of which could flip a raft in a heartbeat. If you took seven of the biggest rapids in the Grand Canyon and lined them up, you would have the Zambezi one-day trip, and the seven-day trip had dozens more wild rapids. There were so many rapids, guides numbered rather than named them, to keep track of which rapid they were heading into.

When I left Zambia midseason to serve as the medic on a trek across Papua New Guinea, I was the only guide who had not flipped. Even though it probably said more about luck than skill, it boosted my confidence.

———

The next spring, Todd, who I had worked with in Zambia, invited me to take part in the first descent of Dream Gap with Whitewater Voyages. This was a remote section of whitewater above Giant Gap on the North Fork of the American River that only a few kayakers had ever run. We hauled the rafts down a hint of trail to the river. They were the first of their kind, self-bailing rafts, which offered the only way anyone could attempt such continuous whitewater. A kayaker had given river notes to our leader, Bill McGinnis, so we were running it on a vague outline of hearsay.

Two dozen Class V guides clad in full whitewater battle gear—wet suits, helmets, sneakers, carabineers, leashes, rescue ropes, and knives—ran in two groups of rafts, leapfrogging one another to each rapid. After one team ran a rapid, they advanced to scout the next. Once they determined the route, they jumped up on a boulder to shout instructions to the oncoming team, who ran the rapid without stopping and went on to scout the next.

While scouting, we quickly evaluated a route and either yelled directions or waved the other team over to come see for themselves. A team running through blind had to make sense of verbal instructions and quickly fit them into what appeared in the oncoming rapid. This provided a whitewater reading class on steroids, dangerous but effective.

We shredded rapid after rapid, stopped for a meager lunch, and pushed on as we planned to finish in one day. At twilight, we came to what Bill hoped was the last rapid, but the notes described two bad rapids just before the gorge opened up—the second more serious than the first. Bill's raft flipped in the first one, and we scrambled to rescue everyone before the second rapid. After the recovery, we climbed the cliff to scout the rapid below.

In the dim light, the rapid looked menacing. A quarter mile downstream where the walls of the canyon opened, a good campsite beckoned, along with our stash of dry clothes and real food. But standing under steep cliffs looking at the worst rapid of the day, having just rescued a flipped raft, its swimmers still cold and wet, we acknowledged it would be foolish to proceed and stopped for the night.

Someone found a small flat area ten feet up a cliff. With quick teamwork, we hoisted a few rafts onto the ledge, made camp, and cooked our emergency freeze-dried concoction off a single burner stove. We flipped the rafts over and arranged our sleeping bags along the inflated floor. It felt like a kid's sleepover, all of us lying in our bags on rafts chatting about the day until exhaustion took over.

After a granola bar breakfast, we looked at the rapid again. The river snaked around a fast S-curve, left to the shoreline, then right into a small pool where the main current flushed left of a boulder into a keeper hole. A steep drop on the right of the boulder seemed to flush through, so coming out of the S-turn in control to make it far right would be possible, but with little room for error.

A portage presented a slog through thickets of poison oak above the cliff. Even in the hopeful light of sunshine, everyone decided to portage—everyone except my friend Todd. He leaned over to me and said, "Frenchy, we can run this." He jerked his head back with a smirk. "We could paddle it alone—just you and me."

Todd was built like superman, a perfect block of granite with a bushy-blond hairdo. They called him Bam-Bam after the kid on *The Flintstones*. He had years of experience on Class V rivers, and I trusted him. It seemed better than dragging the raft over a cliff through poison oak.

"Yeah, let's do it."

We packed the raft with baggage while guides set up downstream with throw ropes. After entering the S-turn, we paddled hard to avoid being swept into the left shore. Todd paddling from the front left was running that muscle machine with a full throttle of adrenaline. I paddled from the back right, but Todd overpowered my strokes. The back of the raft swung toward the left bank, where a tree hung over the river. As we brushed along the shore, a branch caught the rope lashed over our bags. The branch exploded as it snapped the rope and tweaked our angle. Suddenly, the raft pointed left into the worst of the waterfall. We both shouted, "Back paddle!" and fought the current until we reached a micro-eddy beneath the cliff on the right.

We caught our breath for a few seconds. Todd looked back at me as I held onto a nub of rock. He cracked a crooked smile and said, "We can't stay here all day." I nodded and let go. We paddled out of the eddy and dug hard toward the slot, shouting "Yahooooo!" As the raft shot off the lip of the falls, we leaned backward as we feared catching the bow and flipping the back of the raft forward. But the raft slid through, making us heroes for the day.

I basked in the praise from the other guides. They thought I had some expertise, because of my experience on the Zambezi and Todds recommendation. I had no intention of correcting their misconception, and, perhaps, I had finally learned how to read water.

RIVER SPIRITS

In the years ahead, I would run many rivers and absorb their lessons. I scouted rivers by taxi in Turkey, jeep in Pakistan, helicopter in Canada, and bush plane in the Arctic. As my gallery of recognizable patterns grew, my instincts sharpened.

I had been foolish to think I could conquer rapids. The river had slapped me down good my first year and taught me to have some respect. The river was not a highway I could drive along. It had a living spirit. With each river I encountered, my humility transformed further into deep reverence.

After a while, running exciting rapids no longer held such a spell over me. I enjoyed rafting long expeditions on wilderness rivers. Drawn into a half-trance, I could suspend my thinking by observing *li* in the sweep of the currents.

One afternoon on the Alsek River in Alaska, a woman performed a tea ceremony with ice we had collected from Walker Glacier. She moved with grace and care to brew a special green tea. As we sipped from our cups in reverent silence, she said, "I watch the guides gazing at the river all day as they row. Zen masters say that one can draw power from such a concentrated focus on moving water. When we can become one with a powerful body of water and its movement, we become one with its spirit." It was rewarding to hear that the sense of fulfillment I felt reading water had roots in Zen folklore.

It takes time, but the art of reading water eventually becomes both instinctual and intellectual. While scouting, you're thinking and plotting. When you're running the rapid, an unfocused gaze can quickly tell you more about a river than in-depth analysis. Look at nothing and see everything! Not labeling things, but feeling their essence, power, movements and the tapestry of all its elements flowing, braiding, merging, grabbing, bubbling, twirling; feeling the weft and warp of it all and your raft's place in that pattern, finding *li*. Or, like Captain Kirk said, "Just get on the piece of it going your way."

PART TWO
ROWING

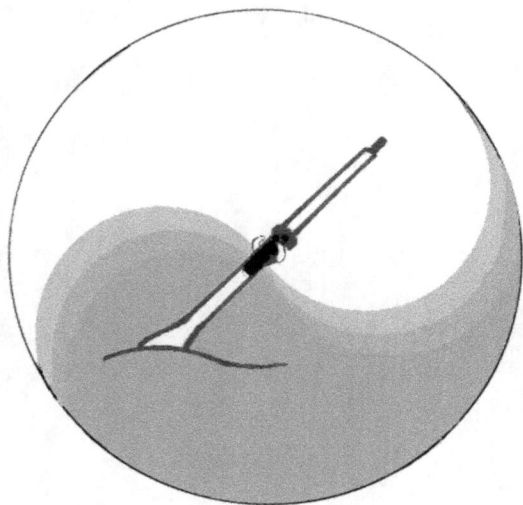

5: DISCOVERING POETRY

Author in rapid Number 18, Zambezi River—photo by Jib Ellison

"Obsession is the wellspring of genius and madness."

— MICHEL DE MONTAIGNE

The general term *boatman* or *oarsmen* denotes both male and female rowers, but it exemplifies the tradition of male dominance in the sport. In my first few years of rowing, it seemed strength was not only a requirement but the best tool for the job. I had not questioned this assumption until the morning I witnessed another type of rowing.

I was emptying buckets at the river's edge at a camp above Dubendorff Rapid in the Grand Canyon. Along came Grand Canyon Dories with their beautiful wooden boats. One by one, they aced the usual route by breaking out of the tongue with powerful rowing over the lateral wave.

The last boat approached the rapid but not down the tongue. It floated straight into a maze of bubbling whitewater and the guide lightly danced her dory through the thick of the boulders and holes. I was smitten by such deft mastery. She had finessed the rapid by moving with *li* and using the river's features. It seemed like her boat melded with the river as I saw her use no powerful strokes in her run. I kept ruminating on that image.

When I mentioned it to Tony, he scoffed at the dory boatmen as spoiled brats who brought cooks along to do all their camp chores, and used volunteers to row heavily loaded rafts to carry all the gear, while the guides rowed lightly loaded wooden antiques. He laughed whenever we saw them waiting for the river to rise so they could run a rock strewn rapid. I listened to my friend's tirade but remained intrigued, wondering how I would ever cross over to that higher realm of rowing mastery.

THE MAGIC OF OARLOCKS

Boatmen can row with either pins and clips or with oarlocks. Pins and clips fix the oar in one position. A stout U-shaped metal clip attached to the middle of the oar slides onto a vertical thole pin on the frame. Many who use pins claim they never miss a stroke because the angle of the blade is set, and the oars usually stay attached if they let go of them.

Oarlocks have U-shaped cradle of stout metal on a shank that swivels in a stanchion attached to the frame. The oars slide into the curve of the cradle. Oars are wrapped where they chaff against the oarlock, and a stopper is set on the wrap to keep the oar from sliding down the oarlock. Rolling the oar in the locks allows the blades to have any angle to the current. Some novices use oar rights to hold the oars in a fixed position in the locks, negating much of the benefit of oarlocks. The advantages and disadvantages of pins verses locks is debated ad nauseam by many highly skilled boatmen. They each have their reasons and stick to them like gospel.

Oarlocks offer a much greater freedom of oar stroke and many more variations of feel for the current. Watch a fish use its fins. It flutters them to catch and release the water as it chooses. With oarlocks, a boatman can release the current's hold on their oar by feathering the oar with a simple flick of the wrist. With pins, you can only release current by lifting the oars out of the water.

When I arrived at the Zambezi River, everyone rowed with pins and clips, which was all I had ever rowed. Many pounded the clips on tight with a rock at put-in to assure they would stay in place when they had to high-side.

On most rivers, guides only used the high-side maneuver when bumping up on a rock, but on the Zambezi River, we used high-siding in many rapids to avoid flipping when the rafts tipped on edge in the explosive waves. We trained our passengers to leap onto the front tube or lunge to the side on command. They could make or break your chance of staying upright. A guide with pins could let go of the oars and high-side, knowing that when he returned to grab his oars, they would probably be there. If a guide used oarlocks, the oars could pop out of the lock into the river when a guide let go of them.

Todd was the first guide I saw row oarlocks instead of pins on the Zambezi. He enlisted my help to do it. One night while everyone was asleep in the warehouse, we selected the two straightest wooden oars, wrapped the shafts and created stoppers with webbing and fiberglass. In the morning, our manager grumbled about us taking the best oars for oarlocks that no one else used, but it was a done deal.

Watching Todd row with oarlocks, I felt that such skill was out of reach for a mere mortal like myself. On some rapids, he never took his oars out of the water.

PRACTICE PRACTICE PRACTICE

The next summer I started rowing with oarlocks on the Colorado. In two hundred and twenty-five miles of river, you spend only forty-five minutes in major rapids on a two-week trip. This leaves plenty of river time to learn how to row with oarlocks and feather the blade to that perfect angle, where it floats through the river without resistance.

I persevered through those first Canyon trips. I had to look at the blade before each rapid to make sure it was perpendicular to the river. Rapids weren't much different for me yet, as I still held the oars with a death grip and took them out of the water on the return stroke. But on flat water, I practiced rowing forward or back while leaving the blades in the water on the return of the stroke. The blades would dive or wobble, but sometimes they returned through the water effortlessly. I found a subtlety in grabbing or releasing current with the roll of my wrist. Feathering the blades while rowing those long stretches became my entertainment.

Between Redwall Cavern and Saddle Canyon,

where the sheer limestone cliffs rise straight out of the water and springs trickle from small alcoves laced with ferns, I found riffles where I could surf on lateral waves. With a well-timed stroke, I left the oars floating on the water as the raft glided along the wave into the rapid. I was finally finding that sweet spot, that effortless sensation when the oars have no weight and respond to the lightest touch. On my fourth trip, I was feathering them in the rapids and having a blast. I decided I would row with oarlocks on the Zambezi River.

COMMITMENT

I got to Zambia in late August, the morning after they had run their first one-day trip of the season. Every raft had flipped at least once. They asked if I could guide that day. I found Todd's oars, and rowed with oarlocks, and did not flip.

The crew that year was a dream team of highly skilled young river guides from all over the country. Charlie Ross had taken over management of the operation and moved us from a dreary warehouse in Livingstone to thatched roofed huts that were part of a campground just off the banks of the river above the falls. We had three crews that rotated on a weekly basis: a crew for one-day trips, a crew for the seven-day trip, and a crew that had a week off to visit game parks as part of an exchange program. Spirits were high.

Most afternoons, we gathered at an outdoor bar along the river's edge. We watched the sunset on the river as elephants roamed the islands while hippos and crocodiles plied its waters, as dreamy an African scene as I could imagine. Basking in that view with a cold beer, we would discuss our recent runs and analyze everything from ferry angles to oar strokes to high-siding to rescues to behavioral changes of the river, always searching to improve. Working on the Zambezi became the greatest rowing clinic in the world.

Jib Ellison filled Todd's position. He had rowed with oarlocks on Class V rivers for Whitewater Voyages and possessed exceptional skills. Throughout that season on the Zambezi, we rowed with oarlocks alongside each other for almost one hundred days. It was like following a graceful skier. I mirrored his approach and sought to copy his technique in the rapids.

At first, my determination to row with oarlocks on the Zambezi proved tricky because of high-siding demands. I practiced keeping a grip on my oar handles as I leaned to the high-side. Usually, the oars slid along with me and stayed in the lock as I returned to my seat. If they popped out, there were calm pools for recovery after most rapids. Eventually, the movement became instinctive, and I didn't worry about losing my oars.

Rowing had become an obsession. I rowed every chance I could, skipping vacation time to cover other guides. With Jib's tutelage, I discovered an entire world in the currents that had been escaping my perception when I rowed pins. Jib referred to the art of keeping the oars in the water and finding that magical smooth stroke *the poetry*. Although that poetry of the oar stroke could be elusive, I rarely rowed pins ever again.

6: ROWING TECHNIQUE, AN ANALYSIS

Author rowing Hance Rapid—photo by Bert Sagara

"It's a great art, is rowing. It's the finest art there is. It's a symphony of motion."

— DANIEL JAMES BROWN, *THE BOYS IN THE BOAT*

We were three river guides with more chutzpah than sense, in London on our way to Zambia for the first time. Whiling away our layover day, we stopped to watch a rowing crew glide down the Thames.

"Let's get a boat and row the Thames!" said Jeff.

We found a rowing club and asked to borrow one of their rowing sculls. They laughed. We insisted we were experts because we rowed Class V whitewater. They laughed even harder. So we spent the afternoon drinking in a pub, watching the smooth strokes of the oarsmen on the water.

While rowing crew is a very different sport than rowing whitewater, the terminology dissects the parts to a stroke with clarity.

Catch: A stroke starts with the rower's knees fully bent, shins vertical, in a full compression position. With arms outstretched and body leaning forward from the hips, the oar blade enters the water.

Drive: This is the stroke's power phase. The rower's legs push off, and, as the rower extends their legs, their back straightens gradually as they swing their torso from a forward lean to an upright position. toward the drive's end, the arms bend, pulling the oar handle toward the body. The stroke starts with the legs, and the back and arms join in later.

Finish: The oar cleanly exits the water at the end of the drive, feathering the oar blade by rolling the wrists until it's parallel to the water.

Recovery: The rower pushes the hands forward, extends the arms, and gradually swings the torso forward. Once the hands pass the knees, the knees bend, bringing the body forward into the catch position as the blade squares to the water.

While rowing a sleek rowing shell differs from rowing a raft through whitewater, the four elements of the stroke remain.

ROWING WHITEWATER

The classic technique is great for rowing backward down a long stretch of flat water, but rowing whitewater is a different animal. The leg strength used in the drive in classic technique is not as effective without a sliding seat and is useless when pushing forward. A guide must be ready to move the boat forward or backward. Rowing whitewater often has more in common with boxing than rowing crew.

Siting Position: You need a dynamic sitting position to row effectively. Most martial arts create a solid foundation first, because a solid punch originates in the legs. Finding a solid foundation for rowing is essential. Pulling back is not a problem because you can push off the frame in front of you, but when pushing forward on the oars, it's challenging to find leverage for a powerful stroke.

Find a supported sitting position where you can lock yourself in place. Scoot forward to the edge of your seat. Drop one foot beneath you to brace against the cooler or whatever structure you are sitting on. This will enable you to push from the dropped leg through the hips. Reach the other leg forward to brace against the end of the footwell. Lock the lower portion of yourself in a dynamic way, like riding a horse with legs activated to take the sway of the waves. Only lock in from the hips down, leaving your torso free to lean and twist. Supported by a solid base, your torso can swivel on your core and you can lean forward to press your oars forward and you can rock back to pull. From this position, you can quickly raise your front foot to the frame bar for a bigger pull. Don't put both feet on the bar.

You don't always have to hold this position. In fact, usually you will be more relaxed, but finding this position should be automatic, so you can snap into it when needed.

Pulling: Pulling back follows the classic rowing form, but less extended. You are crouched forward over your thighs, bracing one foot against the footwell or frame. Push back with legs, while flexing the back, and pulling with shoulders, then arms and elbows, then wrists and hands. Like in the classic technique, use your legs first. Feel the flick of the blade as you cock your wrists back to feather the oars at the end of the stroke.

Pushing: Although pulling back is the more powerful stroke, pushing forward is a much more interesting way to run rapids. While pulling back is used for some maneuvers, especially building momentum, pushing forward gives you a clear picture of the rapid and allows for instant response.

Self-bailing rafts have ribbed floors that catch more current than the bucket boats. When the old-timers tried new self-bailing rafts, they found themselves surfing toward their danger even as they pulled away. Rowers had to learn to use that forward momentum. Approaching a rapid sideways allows for either stroke to position the raft before entry.

At the start of the forward stroke, elbows are folded and the wrist cocked slightly back with a light fist around the oar handle. Lean into the oars and punch forward from just below the shoulder. Lean forward slightly before you punch forward with the arm to get the momentum going. Feel the press of the oar handle against your palm. The punch ends with your fist rolling forward, feathering the oar with the flick of the blade like a fin. Roll back, pulling the feathered oars through the water or in the air until your arms cock for the next push.

Move your hands in compact circles for both pushing and pulling. Keep the blades just under the surface on the drive. Avoid digging deep. It's better to take some quick, well-placed strokes than one that goes too deep and can crab an oar, which is when the current takes hold of your oar and pulls it out of the lock.

Avoid getting the oar handles behind your chest or very far above your shoulders. You lose all power and control there. Keep your oar handles in front of your chest unless you are shipping the oars.

It's easier to keep feathered oars in the water for the recovery when you are pushing. To do it well after a pull, you must cock your wrists back severely. If they are in the water, you can feel the pull of current and let go or hold as much as you want with a turn of the wrist. Get in the habit of feathering even when you bring them out of the water, because feathered blades will slice through any waves.

Once familiar with feathering on the push and keeping the oars in the water, you can stand and row. The stroke is not as full, but it is handy for checking downstream from a slightly higher view. Always watch for rocks or shoals that could pop the down-stream oar.

Stroke: The strength you put into the stroke will be determined by the feel of the current. Don't just slap at the water. If you can give yourself enough room and time, start slow and build to the momentum you want. Often you get only a stroke or two, so make those count with sharp, short strokes.

Grip: My first time rowing Colorado River in the Grand Canyon, I gripped the oars so hard, my fingers became swollen and I had to remove my ring with cooking oil and fishing line. I also had a bad habit of letting my thumbs cover the end of the oar handle until I popped an oar on a rock in the Scott River and fractured my thumb.

Leave at least a few inches between the oar handles and don't grip too tight. Don't put your thumbs on the end of the handles. Wrap them underneath.

When a spring skiing accident shattered my left middle finger, they put it back together with a plate and seven screws, and I had to cancel my spring rafting season.

When I was rowing again after three months of rehabilitation, my finger was weak and sore. In the long hours rowing the Tatshenshini and Alsek rivers in Alaska, the Colorado through the Grand Canyon and the Green in Utah, I softened my grip and worked on the energy transfer from my body into the oar stroke.

Pushing the oars forward against my palms, I hardly used my fingers at all and pulling back was more of a half grip. I focused on pushing from just in front of my armpit, leaning into the oar and following through with arms and hands. Pulling, I would lean back, then pull the oars, and almost pull myself back up as the oars neared my chest. Both had a way of transferring energy into the stroke with less strain on my hands, while an increased sensitivity in my hands improved my feel for the current through the oars.

Shipping the Oars: Shipping an oar means to tuck it alongside the boat, when it's beached or when it must fit through a narrow slot. It is best to ship your oars with the blades to the front. With the blades forward, you can engage them as soon as the front half of the boat clears the obstacle. Whereas, shipping them back leaves them trapped until you are completely clear. You must anticipate how much time and room you need to get them forward before going through a slot.

If you ship oars back or let go of them altogether, be aware that shipping the blades backward makes the handles fly forward. Make sure your passengers know to stay out of range of that radius.

Sometimes you can cross your oars over the center, but that leaves a fair amount of shaft and blade sticking out, and it blocks your movement in the raft. If you do this when beaching the boat, watch out for another boat coming in and smacking that oar blade, which may whip the oar shaft violently into you, the rower.

Oarlock Setup: When setting up your rowing frame, consider your sitting height, the height of the rowers seat, and the depth of the footwell. Tilt the oarlock ten degrees out from frame. When the oar blade is under the surface of the river, the oar should be at ninety degrees to the oarlock when held in neutral position in front of your chest. The oarlock should have only a half inch of free space to the oar.

Oars: It will be important to find oars that are perfectly straight. The wobble from a warped oar will annoy you and stress your wrists.

Use the Force, Luke: Stand in front of a swinging door. Push it open. Now imagine it's stuck by an obstacle weighing hundreds of pounds. Naturally, you will reposition yourself so you can lean into the door with your weight first and then push with your arms. That is the feeling of rowing from your core: grounding your legs, using your weight, and activating the vital internal energy that animates your body to initiate force. That is what one does in Tai Chi.

7: TAI CHI AND ROWING

Author in Grand Canyon—photo by Duncan Berry

"They say the basis of Taoism, out of which Tai Chi Ch'uan was born, is humankind's attempt to harmonize itself with nature."

— MAGARET EMERSON

While bumming around Maui in 1976, I saw a poster for a week-long Tai Chi camp for $70, including room and board. It was a stroke of luck and fate. I had wanted to learn Tai Chi since the days I drove a taxicab on the night shift in San Francisco, where, in the early morning hours, I watched Tai Chi practitioners move in graceful slow motion.

Tai Chi was heavily influenced by Taoist philosophy, particularly the principle of yin and yang, which is the recognition that opposites are both polar and interdependent: dark and light, hard and soft, hot and cold, inhale and exhale, male and female, life and death. One cannot exist without the other.

The yin-yang symbol, called *taijitu*, shows two teardrop shaped swirls that represent the conversion of yin to yang and yang to yin. As one increases, the other decreases. The dot of the opposite field in the teardrop shows that there is always yin within yang and yang within yin. Each holds the seed of its inevitable opposite. Tai Chi uses the natural transition of yin to yang by absorbing and propelling *chi*, the vital life force that flows through everything.

The Tai Chi camp was held on a beautiful bluff over the ocean surrounded by rainforest. For a week I ate vegetarian meals, slept in a tidy bunkhouse, and took four classes a day with Master Benjamin Lo, who had been a disciple of Cheng Man-Ch'ing.

Tai Chi is called an internal martial art, characterized by softness and emphasis on redirecting incoming force. It originated in thirteenth-century China, when Taoist sage Chang San-Feng retreated to Wudang Mountain for meditation. He became inspired when observing a crane attacking a snake. The snake stayed poised, avoiding the crane's relentless attacks, until the perfect moment when it struck with precision, delivering a fatal bite. This encounter led him to develop a sequence of seventy-two Tai Chi postures.

A practitioner of Tai Chi moves slowly through postures with such names as White Crane Spreads Wings, Snake Creeps Down, Single Whip, Cloud Hands, Golden Rooster Stands on One Leg, Parting the Horse's Mane, Brush Knee, Playing the Lute, Repulsing the Monkey, Grasping the Sparrow's Tail, and others that mimic natural form. Moving in slow motion allows one to isolate movement and improve balance. Legs should feel rooted in the ground like an ancient tree, while the torso is as flexible as a sapling.

Every day in that wooden gymnasium, with the sound of palm trees brushing in the wind, my legs burned as we held each posture for Ben to come by and correct us. Holding those positions for more than a few minutes became torture. When Ben wasn't looking, I would shake my legs out and reposition. When he came to me, I felt a gentle touch to make sure my back was straight with my tailbone pointing to the earth and my head floating to the sky. He would loosen the tension from my shoulders, straighten my fingers, and press down on my hips for me to sink lower.

I was no stranger to learning such things. My mother had been a dance instructor, and she taught me tap dancing and ballet. Sports played a big part of my childhood. I had been practicing yoga since my late teens, and for the previous few years, I had trained as an actor in fencing, dance, mime, and a host of other disciplines.

In twenty-four classes over a week's time, we learned a little more than a third of the Yang style short form, or about thirteen postures. Such was their attention to detail and perfection.

Plumbing the depths of Taoism and Tai Chi proved as ephemeral as grasping smoke. I returned to Master Lo's studio in San Francisco many times after that to learn more and refine my form. I discovered that minute adjustments in the shift of weight or the tilt of the hip could bring surprising results.

Living in the huts and rowing one-day Zambezi trips, I had time each morning to practice Tai Chi. The sensitivity I was developing in my hands for rowing had been building in my body for years. I was only beginning to realize how connected the practice was to rowing.

If reading water is about seeing patterns, rowing is about feeling them in the current against the oar blade, and applying the right force at the right time.

Tai Chi is about sensing force, absorbing and redirecting it.

THE PRINCIPLES OF TAI CHI FOR ROWING

Relax

In Tai Chi: Relaxing is easier said than done. Finding every nook and cranny of tension and releasing it takes a particular awareness. Stretching helps, but it is mostly a mental permission to release the tension that can allow the body to let go. Breathe out and let the tension go with it. Quiet your mind and calm your body. This is the preparation for Tai Chi. Every movement should be performed with ease and comfort, not striving and straining. Use no extra muscular effort. It is not being a limp noodle, but using the minimal amount of strength to move from posture to posture with grace.

In rowing: While a sense of urgency common in running rapids inspires using all your strength, use just enough and save the strain. Relaxing the body calms the mind, just as calming the mind relaxes the body.

Separate Yin and Yang (empty and full)

In Tai Chi: Each leg empties as the other takes all the weight, like pouring a pitcher of water from one leg to the other. With one-legged stances, make sure the other leg is weightless. A foot does not fall into place. It lightly touches the ground and fills with weight, like carefully walking across a frozen lake.

In rowing: After expelling all the power out of a stroke (yang), as you draw the oars back on the recovery (yin), think of gathering energy back into your center to roll out again into the next stroke, like a great wave building to break again. This sequence can deliver more than the sum of its parts.

Turn the Waist

In Tai Chi: Movement initiates from the legs and is directed by the waist or, more specifically, from the dantian, a spot four fingers below and two fingers in from the belly button. Everything flows from there. The arms never initiate movement. Movement ripples from the dantian through the back, shoulders, arms and wrist to the fingers. Imagine the movement of a whip. A flick of the arm and wrist sends energy rippling through a loop in the whip to the fringe of the cracker where its velocity reaches the speed of sound. Think about that for generating power!

In rowing: Although you are not standing on ground, you can brace your legs into a solid base and still move from the dantian. Draw chi into the dantian on the recovery and release it from the dantian on the drive. This adds power that merely rowing with the arms cannot match. I have seen guides locked in from the chest down, struggling to push power into their oars with just shoulders and arms. I also saw some blow out their shoulders.

Try this exercise: Stand still and lock your hips in place. Try punching without moving your waist. Now sway to the right and left leading from the dantian, while letting everything else relax and follow. Your arms will swing right and left and practically wrap around your waist with little effort. Now throw a punch starting from the dantian, and feel the difference. Moving from the dantian is the essence of grace and the secret of power.

Body Upright

In Tai Chi: Stay vertically aligned. The tail bone sinks toward the earth as the head floats toward the sky. Don't lean into postures.

In rowing: You must lean forward and back and even side to side. Your torso can be very dynamic, but alignment can help relaxation and deliver energy. Keeping the body aligned and braced helps deliver power. I've seen too many guides knocked back on their seat or try to row from behind their center of balance with little effect. Don't fall far behind the vertical line from your tailbone to top of your head.

Relaxed Wrist

In Tai Chi: Hold the hand flat with the thumb aligned by the fingers. The wrist is straight and relaxed. Don't impede the energy flowing through the wrists and hands.

In rowing: Your wrists do a lot of work and you need to cock your wrists and then roll them forward, but a softer grip will help prevent overuse and injury.

Two Person Push Hands Practice

In Tai Chi: The practice of push hands involves the art of sticking energy, by engaging in contact with the opponent and sticking with that contact while yielding, blending, and redirecting force rather than opposing it. Two players face off with one pushing against the other's forearm, and then they switch seamlessly. Push hands focuses on the ability to adapt, flow, and harmonize with the movements of an opponent, sense any tension or imbalance, and use that point to uproot them. If you doubt the power of Tai Chi Ch'uan, watch the video of Cheng Man-Ch'ing as seven men press on his forearm. He barely moves, but a ripple of energy tosses them all across a room.

In rowing: This is exactly the sensitivity and power one strives to develop with oars and currents. The concept of sticking energy influenced how it felt to leave my oars in the water. Like a hand on the back of a dance partner, I could monitor the energies beneath the water and synchronize my movements with it.

When I started, I rowed like a paddlewheel. I just churned away forward or backward no matter what the currents were doing. With more sensitivity, I didn't fight current as much as use it, timing my strokes with a wave, trough, or eddy line, and, gradually, I extended my awareness to sense each oar separately.

I met many other great rowers over the years and came to see how most used these same techniques. They may not have thought of these techniques in the same way or even thought of them at all, but I can tell a good rower from a mile away.

I rowed dories in the Grand Canyon with some legendary guides who understood the poetry of rowing. Rowing a dory was a guide's delight. The boat skyrockets off waves. As long as you are square to waves you're golden. Dories are narrow with the hard chine and more prone to rolling over than a raft, but what a great ride!

One day, we were finishing up lunch with our rafting group above 209 Mile Rapid in the lower Grand Canyon. Along came the Grand Canyon Dories with their beautiful wooden boats all bobbing along in the midday sun on a clear green river. We had a full view of the rapid from river-left looking down the heart of the rapid as it bent sharply away from us and funneled down to a crashing hole that spanned most of the river. Normally, rowers pull early and hard toward the left shore, but the river bounces back off that gravel shoal, making the breakout move an exhausting exercise in futility because you end up barely missing the hole anyway.

Regan Dale, rowing the lead boat, gave a small nod toward us and lined up on the inside of the river's bend on river-right. I knew at higher levels there was a run down the right, but not at this level. What was he up to?

As he floated along the right shore, Regan squared his boat to a long diagonal wave that ran from the right shore to the front of the hole. He took one stroke and surfed that wave all the way across the rapid to slide left of the hole. As the other boats battled their way through the usual run, we whistled and clapped for Regan's performance. Poetry!

PART THREE
RUNNING

CHAPTER 8
8: LISTEN

Nyami Nyami pendant—photo by author

"The river has taught me to listen; you will learn from it too. The river knows everything; one can learn everything from it."

— HERMANN HESSE, *SIDDHARTHA*

Crocodile teeth and a jawbone tumbled out of my paper sack into the Zambezi River and bounced along the streambed, dancing with bits of gravel until they disappeared.

I hoped my offering would appease Nyami Nyami, the river god of the Zambezi. Depicted as part serpent and part tiger fish, he ruled the river between Victoria Falls and Lake Kariba where a dam had separated him from his wife. Throughout the canyon, his power rippled beneath the water, swirling currents at the flick of his tail, and unleashing his fury in a spray of whitewater.

Every day Nyami Nyami batted our rafts about like swatting flies. He might surf a raft on a wave and spin it around, or catch it in a reversal and shake it like a rug, or flip it into the air with a corkscrew twist, or sink the stern under the bow, turning the raft inside out. If California's rocky rivers were like jazz, and the Colorado River through the Grand Canyon like a symphony, the Zambezi was heavy metal music. Its waves assaulted the boat with the force of a cannon, blowing off hats and glasses and throwing riders to the floor. Guests and guides alike flew out of rafts like hot popcorn. Rowing the Zambezi felt like a daily boxing match with a champion prizefighter.

Every guide on the Zambezi paid homage to Nyami Nyami by carrying a carving or wearing a pendant. In everyday life, none of us would profess to be superstitious, but luck proved as important as skill to survive the one-day trip without flipping or swimming, so we clung to rituals to boost our confidence and to superstition to give us belief. Superstition ran deep. Most Zambezi guides went so far as to not eat crocodile meat in hopes of reciprocity.

Four days earlier, when kayaking with Jib, I had found that crocodile jawbone in a dry wash below Rapid Number Nine. A friend in the States wanted exotic teeth for his necklace, so I took it back to my hut, where I wrenched a few teeth out of it. The next day, I stripped everyone out of my raft, and the day after that, flipped my raft. I had swum Rapid Number Seven three times in a row, if you count my swim from the kayak. Although not unusual by Zambezi standards, it rattled me as I had only flipped once before in two seasons.

Probably more relevant than taking the jawbone was the fact that I had changed my approach to Rapid Number Seven. Mike Grant told me he was pushing his raft through the big diagonal entrance wave. Everyone pulled over that wave backward.

"You don't need power," Mike said. His wide grin served as an enthusiastic call to action. He leaned in and said, "There's a soft spot on the diagonal wave."

Interpreting his description into a split-second maneuver proved elusive. My first two tries had ended with everyone in the water. Was it beyond my skill? Was I being reckless?

After returning the jawbone to the river, I sat

cross-legged and chanted until it resonated through me. When I stopped, the sounds of the river flowed into the silence of my mind. I will never know if it was Nyami Nyami or my subconscious that whispered *listen*, but that word held a deeper meaning for me.

Years earlier, chanting in a field at sunset, my mind wandering around the landscape like a curious monkey, I heard a strange bird song. I stopped and listened for the call. My mind went silent, my senses opened, and the sounds of the nearby forest washed through me. I heard the breeze in the grass. I felt like I heard the clouds scudding past. I was not thinking anything, and that was a revelation. I couldn't listen and think at the same time. My mental monkey was silent, my worries at bay, and my mind on hold.

So for the river to tell me *listen*, it was telling me to stop thinking and let go. My thinking had pushed away listening. Rowing the story I had heard about the rapid blinded me to seeing what it was doing in the moment.

I decided I would let go and listen deeply to the sounds of the river, not think, and see if I could find the key to running Rapid Number Seven. Maybe if I listened deeply enough, the river would show me the way. I rubbed my carving of Nyami Nyami that hung around my neck three times and left the river's edge.

I walked the road to Victoria Falls and practiced listening to the muffled thud of my sandals, the occasional scrape of pebbles, the chatter of the monkeys in the trees, the distant rumble of Victoria Falls.

The path down to the river passed through dense vegetation. Leaves brushed my shoulder. A chain of carabiners jangled against my chest with each step. The drumbeat of crashing waves grew louder until I stepped into a cool amphitheater of rock confining the Zambezi River.

At the top of a hundred-yard-long eddy of angry water known as the Boiling Pot, porters were rigging boats and shuttling gear strewn over the rocks on shore. Snippets of laughter mingled with the pulsing roar of the river. I picked my way over the jumble of jagged basalt.

"*Muli bwange* (how are you), Simon," I called.

"*Nidile bwino, zikomo* (fine, thanks)," he replied.

"Were you dancing last night?"

"Oh yes." Simon flashed a wide, white smile. "All night!"

The eddy was restless. The boats jumped and rocked and pulled at their lines like horses trying to break free. I put on my life jacket, belted my knife over it, and bounce-walked over the tubes into the center of the raft, which lurched at my arrival.

I checked each knot, rope, and strap; adjusted the height of the cooler/seat; and crawled around the oar frame, tightening each screw. The key clicked into the metal, which squeaked tight. The oarlocks rattled as I adjusted their angle and tightened them.

The oars slid into the locks with a thud. I tied my baseball cap to my lifejacket and tightened the strap on my sunglasses. Sitting on the cooler with a sigh, I took a long drink from my water bottle, tightened the cap, clipped its strap around the frame and jammed it into a slot by the cooler. Closing my eyes, I listened to the river rushing past, as the canyon walls made an echo chamber of the river's tones and tempos.

Soon, six clients assigned to my raft took my focus. I showed them where to sit and how to hold on. We practiced high-side drills and the forward lunge where I choreographed the front four clients into a rugby scrum to bash onto the bow on command. We practiced until they could feel the lurch of the raft when they hit it in unison. High-siding was critical to a successful run. The drills also loosened everyone up and made them feel part of a team, attacking the rapids instead of just going along for the ride.

As I returned to my listening meditation, the clients blurred into hazy peripheral shapes, while the river took my focus with its stereophonic symphony.

The guys on shore untied my boat from the cliff. I gave a nod, and they pushed the raft into the grip of the first rapid. I floated on a world of sound: the creak of the oarlocks under the slam of the oar, the watery explosion of the raft breaking through cresting waves, the sparkle of sound breaking all around me with each crashing wave, and my own disembodied commands, "Lunge! Over left! Back to center! Lunge!"

That day on the Zambezi River I was able to suspend myself in a listening place and run the river I found in the moment, not the river I remembered from the day before, or maneuvers others had told me about, or my fears of what if. I was listening to the river and by doing so I experienced the river in a deeper way, feeling symmetry in the confusion of waves assaulting me, calmly sensing the empty spaces, leaning into the soft parts of waves and slicing through. My oars felt like fins stroking the currents swirling in another dimension under my raft.

When I got to the crux move at Number Seven, I felt in tune with the river. I pushed onto the current, sliced through the diagonal wave and slipped into the sweet spot. The river opened to me and gave my raft passage without resistance. Two consecutive waves crested over my raft, first from the right and then from the left. My raft shot through them like a surfer riding the barrel, and I floated out the bottom of Rapid Number Seven as dry as I had entered.

That experience didn't just crack the code to Number Seven, it forever changed the way I approached rapids. Rowing felt less like a battle and more like a dance, listening to the response of another body without thought, in another realm of senses. Since that day whenever I said to myself, *listen*, my inner turmoil quieted, leaving me space to experience the rapid and life for what it was at that moment.

9: FEAR AND FLOW, AN ANALYSIS

Author in Hermit Rapid—photo by Duncan Berry

"Fear makes the wolf bigger than he is."

— *GERMAN PROVERB*

While the majority of time on a river is spent rowing mellow current, there comes a time when a rapid challenges you. Many rowers live for that moment and some dread it, but all have to deal with fear when they encounter it. Fear is a necessary part of the equation. What you do with it makes all the difference.

During my second year rowing the Zambezi River, a videographer accompanied our trips and showed us clips of our runs in the most challenging rapids. Watching those playbacks, I saw a slight difference in the guides who flipped their rafts frequently. They flinched. It was subtle, but in the moment before the first impact, they hesitated. Getting pounded in big whitewater is intimidating and the more it happens, the more it scares, and the cycle compounds. They were getting hammered where others passed through. All the guides were certainly fit and knew how to row. The primary difference was their attitude. There appeared to be a boldness in those who attacked the rapids instead of praying for mercy. One of the most fearless guides was Kelly, who would leap about the boat like a cat and return to her oars without missing a beat.

FIGHT, FLIGHT, OR FREEZE

Facing a big rapid can trigger a physiological response called fight, flight, or freeze. This reaction prioritizes essential functions for survival, such as increased heart rate, heightened senses, and redirected blood flow, which can lead to changes in perception. Three conditions characterize this phenomenon.

Tunnel Vision: This narrowed focus results in a diminished awareness of surroundings. In life-threatening scenarios, humans prioritize actions necessary for survival, like fleeing danger, fighting back, or freezing in place. However, this tunnel vision can blind them to what's happening around them, disrupting their ability to process the full context.

Time Dilation: Some individuals experience a distortion of time perception during high-stress situations. Events may seem to happen in slow motion or very quickly.

Cognitive Overload: Stressful situations can overwhelm the brain with information and trigger a flood of neurochemicals. This cognitive overload impairs the ability to process and retain information, leading to a lack of awareness about one's surroundings or the broader context.

Of these three conditions, cognitive overload is the most debilitating. During a dangerous rapid, you will naturally experience the other two conditions, but if your mind is too jumbled to meet the challenge, you will probably freeze or at least hesitate when action is needed.

Dangerous sports dance with fear. In some, you

only need to get over it initially, like when bungie jumping, but in rowing whitewater, you must grapple with it from beginning to end, which is the attraction of the sport. A successful run is a rush! The desire for adrenaline draws people to a sport like whitewater rafting, and many increase the danger level to heighten their thrill, but that rush requires just the right amount of fear for optimal reward. With the right combination of challenge and skill, some feel they are in the zone or enter what is called a state of flow.

FLOW

The fight, flight, or freeze condition is very close to what athletes and artists consider as performing in a state of flow where everything seems effortless.

The Feeling of Control: A state of flow brings a sense of heightened control over one's actions, but this control is not about domination. It is a state of control without controlling. This state of consciousness allows exceptional pattern recognition.

Effortlessness: Flow involves flexibility and ease. Decisions arise spontaneously from the demands of the activity without deliberate reflection, giving the impression of effortlessness, even if the activity appears strenuous from the outside.

An Altered Perception of Time: In a deep flow state, one's normal perception of time is distorted; it can feel condensed or expanded. Timelessness is a hallmark of the flow experience.

Loss of Self-consciousness: Complete involvement creates a state of unity, where there is no separation between the performer and their actions as self-consciousness disappears.

The fight, flight, or freeze response and the flow state share some of the same physiological and psychological impacts: heightened arousal, focused attention, physiological changes, neurochemical activity, loss of self-consciousness, and efficiency in performance. Both states leverage body and mind capacities to enhance efficiency, albeit for different ends: survival in the case of fight, flight, or freeze , and optimal experience and performance in the case of flow.

One's level of fear seems to be the deciding factor between the reaction of fight-or-flight-or-freeze and the state of flow. Can one contain the fear and turn it into flow? There are some prerequisites for finding the flow state.

Clarity of Goals and Immediate Feedback: Running a rapid offers this in spades. You will know immediately if you have succeeded.

Balance Between Skills and Challenge: The difficulty of a task must provide the right level of challenge to a person's abilities. If it's too difficult, the person will feel frustrated and, if it's too easy, they'll experience boredom. Flow occurs in the sweet spot between these extremes. Take on challenges at or just above your skill level.

A High Level of Concentration: You must find the clarity of mind to combine deep focus with situational awareness. Concentration allows a person to fully immerse in an activity. But it is not a brow-furrowing effort of concentration. It's more about being fully engaged in the moment. The biggest obstacle to concentration in a big rapid is excessive fear triggering cognitive overload.

CONTROLLING FEAR

Whitewater rafting is an inherently dangerous sport. That's the attraction. The fear is not irrational, but there is a difference between logical fear and debilitating anxiety. Fear is part of the game, because the adrenaline rush won't happen in a routine run. In most rapids, fear is minimal and what you feel is just pure exhilaration, but I would suggest that the thrill of a great ride still resides in some amount of danger, even when you don't feel obvious fear.

Of course, what is a joyride for some proves terrifying for others. The responsibility of rowing whitewater is not for everyone, and, normally, no one is forced into rowing rapids. Although, I encountered such a situation once.

In Pakistan, an outfitter wanted to use his mountain guides as river guides in the off-season. The owner called all his guides together and asked, "Who among you knows how to swim?" Twelve mountain guides raised their hands, not knowing what was in store for them.

They hired my good friend, Mike Speaks, to explore the mountains of northern Pakistan for possible whitewater runs while training those new river guides. I joined them a few seasons later when they were to graduate to Class III whitewater. The group had been whittled down to six guides, and only three of them were keen on it in any way. The most fearful one, when approaching a small rapid, simply rowed upstream screaming, "Amirla in trouble! Amirla in trouble!"

We explored a Class V river with the three best guides in my paddle boat. On the last day of the trip, the other students joined us for some big rapids. Mike was rowing with two of the doubtful guides paddling in front and my wife riding in back with a local photographer. She asked him what those guys in front were chanting at the top of their lungs. He replied, "They are reciting the names of their children because they are afraid they will never see them again."

Unlike those reluctant river guides, you signed up willingly and want to row whitewater to the best of your ability by taming any inherent fear, so you don't end up like Amirla.

Build Confidence: Training, experience, and confidence can help you manage your fear of rapids. The more times you run a rapid, the more manageable your fear will become. If you have never run a particular rapid, it helps to watch how others row it to understand that you have made all those moves before. It can also help to follow another boat, but while this is helpful at the entrance, it is difficult to shadow another boat in complex rapids.

The more you run rapids and the more tense situations you conquer, the higher your confidence level will become. You must boost your confidence even if you have to fool yourself into it. That will allow a transformation from fear to flow. The threat is real, but so are your skills. This is the Jedi mind trick you must perform on yourself.

Tame Fear: You can manage fear in the moment by breathing deeply into your belly, grounding yourself, and lowering your center. Inhale through your nose and exhale through your mouth, releasing the tension that fear was creating, and you were holding. A few long breaths should reduce overwhelming feelings. If you have previously practiced meditation and breathing techniques, results will manifest quickly.

There will still be fear, but you can manage it. Don't let it rise from your gut to shoulders and head where it will run wild and take over your thoughts. Instead of thinking of fear as an enemy, transform it into energy. Fear can become, if not a friend, at least an associate. Hold your fear down in your gut like a simmering teakettle, poised to be released in the explosive actions of your run. Fear will stimulate adrenaline, which can sharpen your senses and increase your strength.

Quiet Your Mind: Don't give your anxiety any oxygen. Quiet the chatter of the conscious mind by focusing on whatever physical actions you are taking. Once you are in the rapid, you will be so busy in the moment that fear will recede. This process can open awareness, improve reactions, and perhaps open the doorway to the state of flow.

Let Go: The subconscious can process information faster than thought. To achieve that pure connection with action, you must let go, disconnect yourself, and eliminate the observer. The main principle of Taoist philosophy emphasizes letting go and being present in the moment.

WU-WEI

Wu-wei means effortless action. It means being at peace in difficult situations so that one can act with maximum skill and efficiency, action that does not involve struggle or excessive effort.

Take it from the great martial artist, Bruce Lee. "Wu means not or non and wei means action, doing, striving, straining, or busying. However, it doesn't really mean doing nothing, but to let one's mind alone, trusting it to work by itself. The most important thing is not to strain in any way. During sparring, a gung fu man learns to forget about himself and follow the movements of his opponent, leaving his mind free to make its own countermovement without any resistance and adopts a supple attitude. His actions are all reformed without self-assertion; he lets his mind remain spontaneous and ungrasped. As soon as he stops to think, his flow of movement will be disturbed and he is immediately struck by his opponent. Every action, therefore, has to be done unintentionally, without ever trying."

Like Bruce Lee in combat, rowing a rapid can feel like sparring when you're rolling with the punches and timing your strokes. I prefer to think of it as dancing with the rapid. No matter which metaphor you prefer, the rower needs to stay spontaneous and clear-headed to swiftly identify the characteristics of a rapid and respond effectively.

If the key to finding flow and having successful runs in rapids is a mental state of calm, clarity, and focus, how does one cross over into that condition? Look at what athletes do to trigger a state of mind that invites flow: the ritual. Running a rapid is a high-pressure event. Anything that can help calm the mind and boost confidence is worth a shot.

CHAPTER 10
10: THE WARRIOR PREPARES

Author in the fifth wave of Hermit—photo by Duncan Berry

"Most battles are won before they are fought."

— SUN TSU, *THE ART OF WAR*

Y ou might say pre-performance rituals are all in the head, but isn't that where the battle exists? Studies have shown that rituals help reduce anxiety and improve performance. Whether physical or mental, these routines help athletes and artists feel confident and ready to perform.

I don't know what rituals other guides maintained, but they would have been very subtle. No one wants to see a guide on their knees praying to a higher power for a good run. Your ritual should be personal and have meaning for you.

Before you have even touched the oars or scouted that first rapid of the day, you can prepare yourself mentally and physically. Put at ease as many variables as you can to narrow your concentration to the task at hand when you get to the rapids.

Begin your day by stretching and meditating. Don't plan or strategize. Just be present. Body and mind ready? Check.

Rig your raft for a flip so that everything would still be secure when you flip it back up. Ensure nothing will obstruct your movement. Take your time to balance the load, taking into consideration the distribution of your passengers and make everything bomb proof. Raft ready? Check.

Place your passengers to distribute their weight. If

you have paddlers, review your commands and show them how to ship their paddles and grip the perimeter line with one smooth movement. Make sure the ones in the stern hold on in front and behind themselves. Drill everyone on high-side maneuvers so they know where to go and what to grab onto. Passengers ready? Check.

Once on the water, lighten up, enjoy the scenery and your passengers. Breathe deeply. There is nothing to worry about until you scout the first big rapid. When you get there, take it slow. Don't get injured climbing to the scout rock.

When looking at a big rapid, take in the whole of the rapid from the shoreline to the tongue. What is the speed in the tongue? Where does it flush through the major drops? How powerful is the current? Which eddies could you catch? If you are aware of the overall structure of the rapid, you will have options in the back of your mind for the unexpected.

A big rapid can be intimidating to study, cluttering your mind with thoughts of what if. Talk with the other guides. You may not all be running the same route, but you should all share the same plan as far as running order and who sets safety and where. This is another thing solved and put away in your mind, so you can focus on your run.

Plan your route so each move is the best preparation for the next and uses the features instead of fighting them. Once you have visualized running the whole rapid as efficiently as possible, you are ready. This is important: You must have a clear mental picture of a successful run. Solid plan? Check.

When you walk away from scouting, you enter the final phase of your ritual, which started hours before.

MY RITUAL

Discussions and jokes with the other guides are over. I have decided on my route. It's usually the same as the others, but it will be mine alone when I'm running it. On my return to the boat, I walk as close to the river as I can get and memorize each critical juncture from river level until I am above the rapid, but can still see the entrance. It's easy to get lost when you are being swept into the rapid if you don't have a clear vision of each marker, especially the entrance. If I have to wait for other guides, I stay by the rapid and focus on my breathing. Then I take a last look at the entry.

Back at the boat, I secure everything except my water bottle. I put my sunglasses in my baseball cap and set them down. I get into the river by the boat and lower myself in and tip my head back, submerging into the cold shock. I pop back up quickly, but then do it again even slower and feel the cold seep into my bones. This serves several purposes. It acclimatizes my body to the river temperature, so I will be less likely to flinch away from a big splash, and, if I swim, it won't be such a shock. It completely wakes me up and wipes clean all the trivial details that may have been lingering in my head, while signaling to my body that it's showtime. On cold days, or on icy rivers, I just splash some water on my face and neck like a sharp slap in the face.

Back in the boat, I take my time putting on my shirt or paddle jacket, sunglasses and hat. I fasten a flip line of six-foot webbing around my waist with a locking carabineer. I put on my life jacket with my river knife and take a deep drink from the water bottle before stashing it in the baggage behind my seat.

I scramble up the bank and collect the bow line. A loose rope can cause havoc, and I don't trust anyone except another guide to secure it properly. I coil the rope outward from the raft to the end where all the kinks fall free, wrap the coils, tie it off, and tuck the whole thing under the perimeter rope. I have a passenger hold the boat while I return to my seat. I feel fully ready because, throughout my process, I have relieved my mind of every concern except my focus on this rapid.

After one more quick visual sweep of the raft for anything unsecured, I lift the oars, swing the blades out over the water, check the orientation of the blade, and roll them lightly in their locks as if to warm them up for the challenges ahead.

We would have set the running order during our scout. Trip leader first, followed by the best rower, then everyone else with a solid rower at sweep with rescue gear, first aid and repair kits. After each guide signals they're ready, we row into the current as if the boats were strung together by an elastic band, never getting so far behind that you could not provide rescue, but not so close that you run the rapid together. If there is a paddle raft, it runs in the middle of the pack.

Once away from shore, I rub my Nyami Nyami talisman for a moment while uttering a short Buddhist chant under my breath. All my planning and worrying have finished and I trust that luck is on my side.

I look to my passengers to make sure they are holding on correctly. If they are going to be lunging on command, we practice the lunges. I review with them the sections of the rapid, what to expect and where to swim if they are out of the boat.

Then I say to them, "I know people often ask questions to fill up the silence when they're nervous, but I'll be focusing on reading the river and planning my timing for the run. So unless you have an arterial bleed, don't ask me any questions until after the rapid. Okay? Everybody ready?" I flash a big smile, although my heart is probably pounding through my life jacket.

I open my mind to the river, only concerned with my first maneuver. Each move will lead to the next, and there is no need to think of them until they appear. Adrenaline has primed me to perform, enhancing my senses, making my eyesight sharper and my hearing more acute, but only if I maintain control of it.

So the critical work begins. Relax. Don't think. Find the balance between fear and adrenaline, between surrender and action, somewhere far from the human mind and deep in the river's world. Let the river speak. Listen. Hear the rush of bubbles swirling past the boat, the crash of waves against rock. Feel the surge of current under the raft and use it to dance with the river. All senses are engaged except thinking. I feel the raft responding to the flex of my back, arms, and wrists to the oar as if they are all one.

Currents pulse in webs of energy through the river. Mist blown off the rapid envelops me and the sound of whitewater grows louder, as I row into the tongue. Bam! The first wave baptizes me into action, delivering me into the realm of the river's flow.

YOUR TURN

And now I turn the oars over to you. I will not blab on about all the adventures I had running high water on the Bio-Bio, or lassoing a tree to save boats in Turkey, or exploring rivers in the Hindu Kush, or rowing with icebergs in Alaska.

Now is your time. You know what to do. Go forth and row rivers, discover adventures, make life-long friends, and find divine moments that will grace your life with meaning.

"Carried on the back of Lightning! ... It took me completely. Blood, skin, bones, and memory. I was no longer held fast on earth, but free, fluid, part of the air and sun. ... And so I had my moment of glory, that brief fleeting glory which of itself cannot last. But while it does, it's the greatest game of all." William Faulkner, *The Reivers*

Author rowing through Alsek Bay, Alaska—photo by Bart Hendersen

ACKNOWLEDGMENTS

I want to thank all the guides who shared their wisdom with me: Curt Smith, Jim Slade, Joe Letourneau, Tony Anderson, Alister Bleifuss, Bruce Helin, Mike Speaks, Jib Elison, Mike Boyle, Bart Hendersen, Mike Pratt, Dave Lyle, Craig Corona, Stan Boor, Richard Bangs, Kelly Kalifatich, Jenny Gold, and many more.

Thanks go to all who helped me become a better writer: Willy Bruijns, Peter Gibb, Stanley Toliver, Gail Pearlman, David Widup, Andy Anderson, and especially my wife, Gayle Goedde.

ABOUT THE AUTHOR

photo by Chip Duncan

John French was but one thread in a tapestry of scholars, bums, intellectuals, drinkers, womanizers, feminists, stoners, hippies, punks, and misfits woven into the fabric of adventure travel in the early days of whitewater rafting. Starting on Northern California Rivers, he quickly worked his way into the Grand Canyon crew, and seized an opportunity to guide on the Zambezi River in Africa, which led to running rivers across the globe. What started as a summer job became an obsession as he traveled the world in a quest for the perfect oar stroke, the intimate melding of hands, oars and river on a seam of currents through big whitewater.

Rivers Guided: **North America**: Forks of the American River including Giant Gap & Dream Gap, Merced, Tuolomne, Cal-Salmon, Scott, Kern, North Fork of the Stanislaus, Middle Fork Feather, Colorado, Green, Tatshenshini, Alsek, Tsirku, Kongakut / **Africa**:

Zambezi / **Asia**: Karnali, Bhote Koshi, Gilgit, Ishkomen, Ghizar, Alas, Coruh / **Australia**: Nymboida, Gwydir, Franklin, Snowy, Mitchel, Mita-Mita / **South America**: Bio-Bio, Futaleufu, Upano

---

For more stories from John French visit https://medium.com/@frenchyrio.